I0086386

YOU CAN

21 SECRETS TO GETTING THE

HAVE A

LIFE YOU DESIRE—FULL OF

BETTER

SIGNIFICANCE, JOY AND PURPOSE

LIFE

DAWNA STONE

BAY POINT
media

© 2017 by Dawna Stone

All rights reserved. Except as permitted under the U.S. Copyright Act of 1976, no part of this publication may be reproduced, distributed or transmitted in any form or by any means, or stored in a database or retrieval system, without prior written permission of the publisher.

This book is intended as a reference volume only, not as a medial manual. The information given here is designed to help you make informed decisions about your life and health. It is not intended as a substitute for any treatment that may have been prescribed by your doctor. If you suspect that you have a medical issue we urge you to seek competent professional help.

The book provides advice but does not guarantee any specific outcomes or results.

Printed in the United States of America

First Edition: September 2017
10 9 8 7 6 5 4 3 2 1

ISBN 978-0-9992123-1-8

Edited by Corinne Whiting
Cover design and formatting by Archangel Ink

Trademarked names are used throughout the book. Instead of placing a trademark symbol after every occurrence of a trademarked name, we use names in an editorial fashion only, with no intention of infringement of the trademark. Where such designations appear in the book, they have been printed with initial caps.

Mentions of specific companies, organizations or authorities in this book do not imply endorsement by the author or publisher, nor does mention of specific companies, organizations or authorities imply that they endorse this book, its author or the publisher.

To Dad, With Love

Contents

Introduction: A Wake-Up Call 1

SUCCESS 7

    Chapter 1: Believe in Yourself 9

    Chapter 2: Don't Wait for Success to Find You 17

    Chapter 3: Visualize Your Success 25

    Chapter 4: Be All In! 33

    Chapter 5: Slow Down to Speed Up 39

    Chapter 6: Never Give Up 45

LIFE 49

    Chapter 7: See Life as a Gift 51

    Chapter 8: Practice Self-Acceptance 55

    Chapter 9: Be Your Real Self 61

    Chapter 10: Do What Matters Most 67

    Chapter 11: Forgive Others 77

    Chapter 12: Forgive Yourself 83

    Chapter 13: Learn From Others 87

FAITH 93

    Chapter 14: Have Faith 95

    Chapter 15: Let Go of Fear and Doubt 101

    Chapter 16: Give Thanks 111

FRIENDS & FAMILY 115

Chapter 17: Put Family First................................... 117

Chapter 18: Surround Yourself With Positive People.......... 121

Chapter 19: Become a Passionate Teacher 125

IT'S NOT TOO LATE 129

Chapter 20: Take Care of Yourself... 131

Chapter 21: Live Every Day Like It's Your Last 143

Appendix I: A Better Life Recap 149

Appendix II: Your Chapter Exercise Cheat Sheet ..159

Appendix III: Remembering—A Letter To My Dying Dad...173

About the Author...185

Introduction:
A Wake-Up Call

I thought about calling this book *My Dying Dad*, because that's how the idea was sparked. It took my dad's deteriorating health to awaken and remind me that I wasn't living in the here and now. I wasn't living the life I desired.

So I thought it fitting to title the book *My Dying Dad: What a Dying Man Taught Me About Living*, but my agent wasn't as keen on the idea as me. That's how *You Can Have a Better Life: 21 Secrets to Getting the Life You Desire—Full of Significance, Joy and Purpose* came to be. Call the book whatever you want; that's of little importance. For me, it served as a wake-up call, and I hope it will for you, too.

It's never too late to change your life for the better. *You Can Have a Better Life* inspires you to live the existence you desire and deserve. The book encourages you to stop waiting for success, love and purpose to find you. It prompts you to take action and to live your best life now.

In truth, watching my dad's health rapidly deteriorate pushed me to rethink how to live. But why, I wondered, did it take his looming death to finally wake me up and prompt me to take action? Don't wait another second to make your remaining time worth living. *You Can Have a Better Life* shows how even small shifts in your lifestyle and thinking patterns can welcome in more abundance.

You Can Have a Better Life provides easy-to-follow tips and tools for making your best life attainable. You have a choice. You can continue going through the motions and living a mediocre existence, or you can choose to live passionately with purpose and joy. Simply harnessing the power of free will and taking action can dramatically improve your life and the lives of those around you—allowing you to lead a successful and more fulfilling existence.

You have the power to catapult your success, enhance your relationships, strengthen your love and grow your faith. You'll see the huge impact of incredibly simple changes (that you can start making immediately).

You Can Have a Better Life is divided into five sections. Sections one through four cover "Life," "Success," "Faith" and "Family & Friends." Each section serves as a motivational force to help you live fully—right now!

The fifth section, "It's Not Too Late," reinforces the fragility of life and encourages you to live fully, to stop awaiting the arrival of positive change and to proactively make decisions that create these desired shifts.

Within each section, we will cover the simple secrets to getting the life you desire. You will learn to:

1) Believe in yourself
2) Go after success rather than waiting for it to find you
3) Visualize your success
4) Be "all in"
5) Slow down to speed up
6) Never give up
7) See life as a gift
8) Practice self-acceptance
9) Be your real self
10) Do what matters most
11) Forgive others
12) Forgive yourself
13) Learn from others

14) Have faith

15) Let go of fear and worry

16) Give thanks for what you have

17) Put family first

18) Surround yourself with positive people

19) Become a passionate teacher

20) Take care of yourself

21) Live every day like it's your last

You Can Have a Better Life ultimately teaches you how to willingly receive the goodness that comes your way. Too often we close ourselves off, believing that prosperity is not ours to have. When we block ourselves from those gifts, we miss out on unbelievable opportunities. This book shows you how to create your own change, while at the same time welcoming infinite blessings from the world around you.

The step-by-step guidance will help you remove obstacles and lead you along the right path. Use the exercises at the end of each chapter to ensure you follow all 21 steps designed to create the desired shift.

At the end of the book, you'll find a heartfelt letter I wrote to my dying dad. If you have ever lost someone dear to you, whether or not a father figure, I assume you will, in some way, relate to this sincere outpouring of love. I hope it will motivate you to move toward your desired life before it's too late. It's time to wake up and live passionately with purpose and joy!

Free Gift:

As a special thank you for purchasing *You Can Have A Better Life*, I want to give you two chapters of my next book: *Succeed With Purpose: Unleash Your Potential, Boost Your Career and Increase Your Income.*

To claim your free chapters, go to:
DawnaStone.com/SWPchapters

Although there is no obligation, if you *do* have a chance to read these free chapters, I would be delighted to hear your feedback. You can connect with me at Dawna@DawnaStone.com.

SUCCESS

Believe in yourself! Have faith in your abilities! Without a humble but reasonable confidence in your own powers, you cannot be successful or happy.

– Norman Vincent Peale

Chapter 1:
Believe in Yourself

Are your current beliefs—those you keep hidden deep inside for only you to hear—holding you back? Do you think you're worthy of a better life, with more success, more happiness, more money, a more fulfilling job and more meaningful relationships? You may want these things, but desire on its own isn't enough. You have to believe that you're worthy, and you must also put aside all your fears, all negative thoughts and any beliefs of unworthiness.

The first step to finding success involves believing you are capable of having it. Most of us want more success, but few of us actually are convinced we are worthy or have what it takes. Wanting and believing must work in tandem for success to be found.

I was fortunate to have parents who encouraged me to believe in myself. They made me feel like I was capable of doing anything I set my mind to. I realize how extremely lucky I was to receive this unconditional support and encouragement that so many never experience. However, while it's undeniably great to have others believe in you and offer encouragement, true greatness and success only arrive when you first believe in yourself.

The initial step to finding more success in your life: Believe you're truly capable. Initially, that may not sound so difficult. But if we look deep inside ourselves, we often find that we are the ones sabotaging our own greatness. How often do you hold yourself back? How often do you let fear or another person keep you from pushing forward? How often do you quietly think, "I can't," "That's not possible" or "That isn't going to happen to me?"

You have to decide what it is you really want. I mean *really* decide. Make your desire a focal point in your life. Make all your decisions based on that want. Once you make that determination, you need to focus on that end goal like your life depends on it.

Maybe there's one thing you really want, or maybe you have five, 10 or more ideas in mind. No matter the number, start thinking about these aspirations and, better yet, write them down.

Maybe you want freedom from your boring, unsatisfying job. It's great that you know this, but be more specific. What is it that you hate about your job? Why do you want out? Do you love your boss but hate the long hours that keep you away from your family? Do you make less money than you'd like, do you travel too much, or does your job not sufficiently challenge you?

Now that you know why you want to leave your job, be even more specific. What does your dream job look like? How much will you travel? What type of hours will you work? What kind of commute will you have? What will your boss be like? Imagine your perfect role. This may not be something you can articulate in a few minutes—not if you're being truly honest with yourself (while also being realistic).

Take some time to pinpoint exactly what you're looking for. If you don't know what you want, how are you supposed to get it? Without the specifics, you can't take the necessary steps to move forward and get what you want. I want you to be as detailed as you can when imagining your new situation. Imagine traveling to your job, envision yourself in the position, and picture your new boss and what each day will entail. The more details you can conjure up, the better. In your mind, act as if you have already secured the job.

Once you have a clear picture of what it is you want, start thinking about the steps needed to get there. Again, make sure you're specific. When do you want to leave your current job? How will you leave? How will you find your dream job? Must you have landed your new gig before leaving your current one? When will your new role start? How will you dress on your first day?

Maybe you can't relate to the above example because you love your current situation. Think about something else in your life that you want to change or improve. No matter what it is that you want—a better relationship with your significant other, a promotion or raise, a healthier or thinner body, to start a business or write a book—you need to be specific and deeply consider how you can turn your desire into reality.

And no matter what you seek, you need to assess any limiting beliefs and make them disappear.

I find that a simple exercise can help. I know it may sound kooky and look even crazier, but I promise it works. If you have any thoughts currently holding you back, find a quiet place to sit and close your eyes. Allow those negative and limiting thoughts to surface; when they do, bring your hands to your head and imagine those negative thoughts to be magnetic and your hands the magnets. Now envision pulling all those limiting thoughts from your mind. Every negative thought flows out of your head and into the palms of your hands; when they've all been removed, pull your hands away and toss those thoughts far from you, letting them dissipate into thin air.

This release of negative thoughts or Meditation Release™ will almost immediately make you feel lighter and freer. It'll give you the fresh starting point you need.

You can take this process one step further. After releasing your limiting thoughts, sit quietly with your palms on your thighs, facing upwards and ready to receive. Think about all the positive thoughts needed to succeed presenting themselves to you. Those thoughts can range from "I am capable" to "I am worthy," or anything that you know will help you move forward. As you sit there quietly with your eyes closed and open palms facing upward, imagine these thoughts materializing in the air around you and falling into your expectant hands. Once all the thoughts have stacked up in your open palms, bring your palms to your head and allow these positive ideas to enter your mind. Imagine these thoughts being pulled into your subconscious and becoming part of who you are.

This simple exercise will get you in the habit of purging negative, limiting thoughts and inviting in the positive thoughts to help catapult your success, ultimately giving you the life you desire and deserve. It will also help open your mind and allow you to get the most out of the next 20 steps. Give it a try. What do you have to lose?

Chapter Exercise:

Set aside five to 10 minutes, find a quiet spot, and give Meditation Release™ a try. Do both the release exercise and the receiving exercise. Repeat the exercise daily for at least one week, and then determine for yourself whether you benefit from a daily, weekly or monthly practice. I tend to do the exercise once a week unless I feel as though something is holding me back from achieving my goals; in that case, I may practice daily for a short period of time to help break through my negative thoughts and to embrace the positive ones.

If you want to take it one step further, write down how you feel before and after each session. This additional practice can welcome even more clarity around your thoughts, helping you to focus on those that may catapult you forward rather than hold you back.

The only place where success comes before work is in the dictionary.

– Vidal Sassoon

Chapter 2:
Don't Wait for Success
to Find You

If you've ever thought, "There must be more to life than this," you're not alone. Simply desiring something and believing in yourself isn't enough. Positive change only comes with action. Things begin to happen when you *make* them happen. It sounds simple, because it is simple. If you push ahead, the effort you put forth will begin the forward motion needed to capture success. You'll notice I said "capture." Success isn't going to find you just because you want it. It's not going to seek you out just because you're a good person. It's going to happen when you desire it, believe you deserve it and, most importantly, act upon it.

If you're reading this book, chances are you already want to change your life. You're reading this because you're meant to be hearing these words right now. If you make the choice, this can be the start of your new and better life.

You have the power to succeed because you possess the power of choice and the power of action. It's up to you which direction you want to move; it's up to you to make it happen. You can alter your life by simply moving forward, and I'm not necessarily talking about making a huge shift. Even small, simple actions can make a major difference in your life, finances, relationships, happiness and overall success.

How do you make it happen? We all have the ability of turning something mediocre into something great; we must do only two things—develop a plan and follow it. Creating a plan is the easy part; acting upon it is where most people get stuck.

Early on in my career, I felt so stuck that I not only experienced emotions of despair, but also those of immense hopelessness. I worked at a job that I very much disliked, and I spent four years being miserable. I wanted to do something else and dreamed of finding a job I loved, yet I didn't do anything about it. Every day I would wake up and drag myself to my job. Why? Why would I spend four years of my life doing something I didn't want to do? I look back now and wonder why I wasted all that time, when all I needed was to implement a plan and act on it. Like most people, I was waiting for positive change to find me rather than creating a proactive strategy to go after it.

When I finally decided I'd had enough, I devised a plan for getting a new job that involved updating my resume, researching industries and companies that interested me, writing a cover letter, putting together a list of contacts, etc. The amazing thing was just how simple it was to make that plan. It took less than a week for me to gather all the pieces so that I could start making calls and arranging interviews. The simple act of moving forward in the right direction landed me my dream job in a completely different industry—in the city where I wanted to live.

Because the plan of looking for a new job and the act of actually reaching out and making meetings proved so easy, I often wonder why I didn't begin sooner. Stop waiting for change to find you. Go out, and make change happen.

Where do you feel stuck in your life? Where would you like to see change take place? Do you want to improve your relationship with you boyfriend or girlfriend, your spouse or your kids? Do you want to build stronger friendships? Do you want a new job, or do you want to start your own company? Do you want to make more money and have more freedom to do the things you love? No matter what you're looking for and regardless of how stuck you may feel right now, make a plan. Sit down and write out a list of three to five things you could do that would move you in the right direction. Then under each item, write what necessary action can make that happen.

Here's a real example: Last year I wanted to make sure I was maintaining meaningful relationships with my kids. Although they are still young—I have a 9-year-old daughter and an 8-year-old son—I found myself often so busy that time would pass, filled with nothing but typical day-to day-activities—getting ready for school, getting dressed, feeding pets, doing homework, driving to after-school activities and so on. As a full-time working mom, I wanted to make sure my kids felt that, although I worked, I was there for them. So I made a plan.

Goal: Have a more meaningful relationship with my kids

Plan:

1) Spend quality one-on-one time every week with each of them

    a) Find a chapter book and read every night with Kaelie

b) Make a game out of putting away Luke's dirty clothes, which came to be known as "dirty clothes basketball" (FYI: this was a big hit!)

2) Sit down to dinner together at least three days a week

   a) Turn off the TV and talk about the day. Ask them about school and when they respond with, "It was fine," ask more questions.

3) Say a before-dinner prayer

   a) Make a family ritual of giving a short prayer of thanks before dinner

4) Participate more fully in something they enjoy

   a) Throw the football or shoot hoops once a week with Luke

   b) Have Kaelie teach me new poses she learned at after-school yoga class

5) Once a year, take each for a "mommy and me" weekend

   a) Let the kids pick the location (within reason and within driving distance)

   b) Make it special, and let them help plan the trip/agenda

With the exception of the "mommy and me" weekend, the plan was super simple to develop and act on. I could even take the plan one level further by writing down which weekday each activity will happen. (For example, every Sunday before dinner, I play hoops with my son.) These small behavioral changes made all the difference in the relationships I currently have with my kids. I realize that teenage years can be much more difficult than the pre-teen years, but hopefully the bond I'm creating now will only strengthen our relationship as the kids get older.

Start right now—no matter where you are in your life at this very moment. No matter how stuck you feel or how dire life feels, decide that you will take some daily action; no matter how big or small, that will move you forward.

Quit expecting or hoping, and start acting!

Chapter Exercise:

Start by writing down one thing you want to change in your life. It could be something about your job, your finances, your relationship, your health, etc. Then take a few minutes to record three to five actions that will move you in the right direction. Then take it one step further: Under each item listed above, write a specific action that needs to take place for you to succeed. Set a timeframe for each action, and then schedule it into your day.

Whatever you hold in your mind on a consistent basis is exactly what you will experience in your life.

– Anthony Robbins

.

Chapter 3:
Visualize Your Success

You can't grab what you can't see. How are you supposed to go after what you want if you can't imagine having it? Our thoughts can determine our reality. If we can learn to control our thoughts, we have the ability to create our own reality.

Thoughts are more powerful than you realize. If you have an important goal, directing your thinking toward that aim will help you achieve it. But make sure you're clear about what you want. Imagine yourself achieving it, having it and living it.

To build on that, in addition to harnessing the power of your thoughts, use visualization. You may already know about this effective practice, as many athletes talk about it as the key to their success. But you don't have to be a gold medalist or a football MVP to benefit from this tool.

When I was a young athlete, our coach did visualization sessions with us on a regular basis. I remember the entire swim team finding space on the floor in the pool's storage room. The coach would walk us through a series of steps—the minute before walking up to the starting blocks, stepping up on the block, hearing the starting gun, hitting the water, etc.

Although each of us on the team was a different age, had different skill levels and often swam different events, our coach used generic terms to make sure we could all visualize our particular races. He also taught us how to get more specific in our mind's eye and to "walk" ourselves through every lap—feeling our muscles tense, the water slide over our bodies and our hands hitting the finish wall with a new personal best.

I used visualization throughout my swimming career and then later when I became a triathlete. This tool helped me find success at every triathlon race from Olympic-distance competitions to the Hawaii Ironman. I can confirm that it truly works!

As I got older, I continued to use this valuable tool to help me succeed in other areas; however, it wasn't until a few years ago that I hired a life coach and made my first vision board. For someone like me who has been using visualization since childhood, I didn't think this new-to-me tool would offer any benefit. I'm happy to report that I was wrong! I am now a true believer in the power of the vision board, and I believe that using the two together—traditional visualization and a vision board—is a guaranteed formula for success.

The process of creating one's board can be a fun and valuable experience. My coach instructed me to make a board highlighting the things I still want to achieve in my life. "Be as specific as possible," she said. So I designed a vision board with as much detail as possible.

My husband did the exercise with me, using the old-school method of paper, scissors and glue. He cut out pictures from magazines that represented what he still wanted to achieve. I, on the other hand, used my computer to gather images from websites, "cutting" and "pasting" them into a PowerPoint slide.

I urge you to do this exercise and not worry about what anyone else may think. In fact, there is no need to share your board with anyone. Simply be true to yourself.

So what to put on your vision board? Compile images that carry significance for you. It can be photos of material items you want or images that represent a feeling, a relationship or even a memory you don't want to forget. The finished product can be motivational, spiritual or even whimsical.

When I did my vision board, with each addition, I asked myself, "Is this something I really want?" One challenge can be that—as you sift through photos or images to put on your board—you often come across countless options you like. Take, for example, *Coastal Magazine*—one of my favorite publications. Every time I open that magazine, I fall in love with the featured dream house. There is a part of me that wants to place that beachfront mansion on my vision board. But then I ask myself the true importance of that house; when I'm honest with myself, it's not something I really aspire to. Focus on those things that matter most.

To give you an example, my board features 16 images. Some of those images include:

1) A picture of my kids—to remind me to spend more quality time with them

2) A picture of my husband and me at a fun event—to remember to find the time to have fun, even when we're super busy

3) A picture of a "For rent" sign—to represent my goal of owning a vacation home we can rent out

4) A girl doing a yoga pose—to focus on a regular yoga practice

5) A picture of a literary agent—to keep up my search for an agent

6) A picture of my college girlfriends—to remind me to stay in touch

7) A picture of a cookbook—to inspire me to publish one

8) The HSN logo—to represent my goal of working with this company

To date, I've been able to focus on and achieve all eight of these images/goals. Admittedly, I'm still working on some of the other goals, like trying to relax more, take better care of myself and achieve six-pack abs!

Chapter Exercise:

Set aside an hour of uninterrupted time in the next seven days to create your vision board. Remember to stay true to yourself. No one but you needs to see your work. Once you have your board, post it somewhere you will see it often. If you don't care if others see it, too, I recommend posting it on your bathroom mirror. If you want to keep it private, put it in your sock or underwear drawer where it catches your attention each time you reach in. Most importantly, have fun with the exercise. The activity shouldn't be stressful; it should be motivational.

Once your vision board is complete, make a point of taking just one item from the vision board each day to visualize achieving it. (I suggest right before bed as a great time.) I've found that I can take 60 seconds when I first hop under the covers to do a brief but productive visualization. Remember to make your visualization as specific as possible. Imagine how you will accomplish each goal, see yourself achieving it, and experience the feelings you'll enjoy following your success.

Sometimes success is simply being willing to give it your all.

– Amanda Beard

Chapter 4:
Be All In!

The one thing successful happy people have in common: They are "all in." The topic at hand doesn't matter; it's the passion with which it's done that is notable.

Are you all in? Are you doing everything in your power to move yourself to a place of joy and abundance?

The first time I experienced being "all in" was in 2004. I had just decided to leave my high-paying corporate job and to launch my own company, with the goal of publishing a national women's running magazine. To put things in perspective, although I had in-depth marketing and finance experience, I didn't know the first thing about publishing. In fact, I had absolutely no experience with editorial content, bookstore distribution, subscription management and ad sales—all things that were pertinent to launching a successful magazine. But I chose to jump in headfirst and to give it everything I had.

I spent months researching the industry, having coffee or lunch with other publishers and meeting with printers, distribution companies and subscription management services. Some of the publishers I approached for advice encouraged me to return to my corporate job. All but one encouraged me to give up on my dream, stating that I wouldn't be able to make it work.

I flew to New York to meet with one of the publishers I respected most. George Hirsh, the publisher and founder of *Runner's World*, agreed to meet up and discuss my concept. I was thrilled to meet with someone with such a long and successful publishing career, and George was kind to take time out of his busy day to offer advice. I liked George immediately. He seemed genuinely interested in my ideas. Yet although George offered great advice on how to launch a magazine, as well as how to manage distribution, circulation and advertising, in the end, he advised me to not move forward. He went so far as to say I'd be foolish to think I could launch a successful national independent magazine. His reason for discouraging me? He strongly believed national advertisers would never advertise in a small independent publication.

I'd be lying if I said I wasn't discouraged by all the negative feedback, especially when it came from George. Yet I was so passionate about the idea that I still leapt forward and gave it my all. Don't get me wrong; I listened to the naysayers and heeded their warnings—especially the one about capturing national advertisers. Consequently, I put all my effort into our advertising sales. Equipped with only a sample of the magazine, I set up meetings with as many national advertisers as possible, and something amazing happened. Several of them gave me verbal commitments right there on the spot. They loved the concept and liked the passion I displayed.

Two years after our initial meeting, I ran into George and his wife at an awards ceremony. By this time, my magazine was flourishing and included numerous national advertisers like Toyota, Nike, L'Oréal, Timex, Oakley, Ford, Kellogg's and many more. George's wife had heard about our meeting and when George introduced us, she smiled and said, "I know who you are. Aren't you glad you didn't listen to my husband?" I simply smiled and told her my meeting with George pushed me to go the extra mile to ensure that *Women's Running* became a success, and I would always be grateful for that.

Launching that first company was one of the scariest things I've ever done, but I was adamant about giving it my all and doing whatever it took to achieve my dream.

I'd be remiss if I didn't also admit that being "all in" meant working harder than I ever had before, yet it was worth it. In 2012 I sold the company for millions and still look at the process of building the company as one of my most rewarding experiences.

Do you have a business idea you want to launch? A book you want to write? A charity you want to start? A promotion you want to receive? Are you giving it your all? In order to succeed, you need to be "all in." Success is waiting for you. Give it everything you've got, and go get it!

Chapter Exercise:

Pick an important aspect of your life. It can be your career, a relationship, a personal goal, a skill you're trying to master, etc. Be honest: Are you currently giving this area your all? Are you "all in" or only halfway in? Decide to go for it. Make a list of five actions you can take to ensure you're giving it everything you have. Be all in!

Slow down and enjoy life. It's not only the scenery you miss by going too fast; you also miss the sense of where you are going and why.

– Eddie Cantor

Chapter 5:
Slow Down to Speed Up

It's often important to quiet the mind and slow down before you can speed up and find true success. Yet there's no doubt it can be difficult to find clarity and purpose with so many thoughts running through your head and so many items filling your to-do list.

We are all moving at such a fast pace in our attempts to achieve more that we often forget to pause and analyze what's actually working and what's not. Sometimes the answers to our problems lie right in front of us; we're just moving too quickly to get a good glimpse.

In her book *You Are A Badass*, New York Times best-selling author Jen Sincero tells a story worth repeating. One day while in her California home, a bird suddenly flew in through a wide-open door. Terrified and out of his element, he panicked and started flying into walls and other items around the house. Full of fear, the poor little bird charged full speed at the window over and over again while trying to escape. She writes, "In an attempt to escape, he kept slamming himself into the window while I feebly chased him around with a flip-flop, trying to guide him back toward the open door." Once the bird finally found its way to freedom, Sincero realized the similarities between the bird's reaction and our own. The bird could see outside through the window, yet no matter how many times he tried or how hard he worked, he couldn't get the result he wanted.

She continues, "It made me think of the way so many of us live our lives. We can see what we want, and nearly kill ourselves trying to get it in a way that's not working. Meanwhile, if we just stopped, got quiet for a minute or two, and looked at things a little differently, we'd notice the door to what we want being held open for us by the nice lady in the bathrobe across the room. Then all we'd have to do is fly through it."

Can you relate to this story? I sure can. There have been many times in my life that I thought if I only tried harder or tried again, I'd finally get the outcome I desired. But in reality, I just needed to take a step back, evaluate the situation and make adjustments.

The ability to slow down and analyze your actions may be all you need to find your open door—and to achieve success.

If you're having trouble slowing down, try meditating. A meditation practice can help you get more clarity. If meditation is new to you, try these five simple techniques to get started with your practice:

1) Find a peaceful place (preferably somewhere without distractions).

2) Sit in a comfortable position. If needed, place a towel or blanket under your sit bones to add comfort.

3) Focus on a single point. This can be a candle, a spot on the wall or even a tree.

4) Try and clear your mind. This may be challenging at first. When thoughts enter your mind, simply acknowledge them and then let them go. If you have difficulty controlling your thoughts, try focusing on your breath. Simply saying "in" and "out" as you breath can help clear your mind.

5) Start slowly. You don't have to meditate for an hour to reap the benefits. Begin with five to 10 minutes, and build up to 20 minutes several times a week. Or simply aim for 10 minutes a day. Even a short

period of time repeated on a daily basis can help reduce stress and anxiety.

If you don't currently have a meditation practice, starting one can alter your life. I urge you to give it a try. Even a few minutes a day can calm your mind and provide the clarity you need to succeed.

Chapter Exercise:

Take some time to assess where you are in your life and what's working and what's not. If something hasn't been working, then step back and analyze why rather than simply pushing harder. It may be that your efforts just need a slight shift in direction. By taking a step back and slowing down for a short period, you give yourself the time needed to evaluate the situation, adjust your course and ultimately succeed.

Everyone gets knocked down. What's important is getting back up.

- Mark Burnett

Chapter 6:
Never Give Up

Stop fearing failure. The most successful people fail over and over before they succeed; the thing that sets them apart is that they don't ever give up. Instead, these people learn from their failures, make adjustments and try again.

Take risks, stumble, and get back up again. Learn from your mistakes and push on, until you no longer stumble but instead leap forward and thrive!

Stories abound of well-known personalities who never gave up and finally achieved their dreams. Stephen King, for example, lived in a trailer and was too poor to pay for a telephone while pursuing his writing career. He sold his first short story for a meager $35. Today, King is one of the most successful writers of all times, with a listed net worth of more than $400 million.

Countless other authors experienced rejection and failures before hitting it big. In fact, 12 publishers rejected J.K. Rowling before she received a book deal for her beloved *Harry Potter* series. Margaret Mitchell received 38 rejection letters for *Gone with the Wind*. And according to Jack Canfield, his famous *Chicken Soup for the Soul* was rejected a grand total of 144 times!

Actor and comedian Jim Carrey completely bombed his first onstage performance. But he didn't let failure hold him back. Instead he moved to Los Angeles, honed his skills and became one of Hollywood's highest paid actors (according to *Forbes* magazine).

I'd be remiss if I didn't include Oprah Winfrey in this list, too. Oprah overcame a difficult childhood. As an adult, she became a lauded network anchor who was constantly criticized for her weight gain. Overcoming continuous obstacles and ignoring criticism from the naysayers, Oprah persevered to become one of the most successful and admired women on the planet.

When things get difficult, don't go as expected or suddenly feel impossible, we tend to want to run and hide. In many situations, it's obviously much easier to give up than to persevere. Yet it's those admirable individuals who keep pushing forward and don't give up who ultimately find success—or success finds them.

I almost gave up on one of my dreams. In 2012, I sold both my companies. I had launched the first in 2004 and the second in 2009. After the transaction had been completed and I'd spent a few months helping transition the company to its new owners—a large company based in California—I decided to take some time to finally write the health and wellness book I had been dreaming of for years. But there was more to my dream; I also wanted to get a large publishing house to publish the book.

While writing the book, I was also shopping my proposal and actively looking for a publisher. Yet I couldn't find a publisher willing to give me a deal. The feedback was always the same. The publishers all commented that the concept wasn't unique and didn't have a "hook." You see, my book was simply a step-by-step guide for eating healthier and losing weight. There was no gimmick, as it wasn't a quick-fix plan. But without this selling point, it seemed my book wasn't interesting enough for the large publishers.

I would be lying if I didn't tell you that I found the multiple rejections to be extremely discouraging. But I wasn't ready to quit. So rather than giving up on the dream of publishing my book *Healthy You*, I took a slightly different path.

Instead of shelving the idea, I decided to try my hand at self-publishing. I felt passionate about the book and believed there was an audience for it, so I moved forward on my own. Guess what? My self-published book did so well that the same publishers who initially rejected my idea later expressed major interest in the book. That self-published book landed me a six-figure book deal!

I could have very easily given up on my dream of getting the book published by a large publishing house; instead, I simply found another road that led me to my end goal.

Learn from your failures, overcome your obstacles, and look for alternative paths to your goal. Never give up. Success may be waiting just around the corner.

Chapter Exercise:

Take a minute and think about something you really want to achieve but have encountered obstacles in doing so. Think about the steps you can take to keep moving forward with your dream. And remember, there may be more than one path that reaches your end goal.

LIFE

The biggest adventure you can take is to live the life of your dreams.

– Oprah Winfrey

Chapter 7:
See Life as a Gift

I need to preface this chapter by saying it is the shortest chapter I've ever written and it just may be the shortest you've ever read. There is however, good reason for its brevity. The chapter covers a simple state of mind that can completely change your outlook on life. Although I could try to fill the chapter with unnecessary stories and more words just for the sake of making it more robust, it wouldn't provide either of us any additional benefit. So it remains a very short but critical chapter in the book.

We've all heard the saying "life is short," and I don't think anyone would argue with that statement. But we should also consider life a very special gift.

We are often so busy going through our day-to-day activities that we don't take even a second to step back and realize how lucky we are simply to be alive. More often than not, we emphasize the painful parts of life—loss, sadness, stress—and that negative focus can take over and suck the joy right out of us. Things only become truly rewarding and fulfilling when we recognize life for what it is—a gift.

I, like most people, often forget to be thankful. I get so wrapped up in my daily chores—running my son to basketball and soccer practice and my daughter to gymnastics lessons, doing homework, making lunches, returning phone calls and answering texts, taking meetings and scheduling conference calls—that I miss out on life's true joys. It's not that these tasks aren't important, but during all the craziness, we all need to pause and be thankful for the lives we already have.

If you are reading this book, you are probably wondering how you can improve your life. No matter where you are right now, make a personal commitment to view your existence as a gift and to find more joy today. This personal commitment is a conscious choice that you can fully control, and it serves as the basis for improving your life. Simply realizing that life is a gift will help you build a life that is purposeful, meaningful and joyful.

Chapter Exercise:

Take five minutes and make a list of all the things currently sucking the joy out of your life. Then make another list of all the reasons you're thankful for your life. Take the first list, and just acknowledge each item. Throughout the book you will receive guidance to help you control and change the things draining your happiness. Fold up the list for now; at the end of the book, you can take it out again and use the exercises to help adjust or eliminate each item holding you back.

Take your second list, the "thankful list," and put it somewhere you can refer to it often (or if it's an electronic file, somewhere that's easy to access). For the next few weeks, review the list on a daily or weekly basis. You can even schedule your "thankful review" into your calendar. I'm confident that the simple act of recording your gratitude and reviewing it often (or even adding to it) will give you a more positive outlook on life.

If you can, do this exercise now!

Every thought we think is creating our future. What I believe about myself and about life becomes true for me. What you choose to think about yourself and about life becomes true for you. And we have unlimited choices about what we can think.

– Louise Hay

Chapter 8:
Practice Self-Acceptance

L ove who you are (right now), and be kind to yourself. We are often more critical of ourselves than we are of others. We constantly put ourselves down; by doing so, we slowly slide down the slope of treating ourselves poorly. Over time, we start believing the things we tell ourselves, and those negative thoughts become our reality.

Too many of us dislike ourselves. We might not admit it, but we have self-critical thoughts all the time. We think we're not pretty enough, tall enough, thin enough, smart enough, funny enough… We think we don't make enough money or have the ability to fall in love.

Sometimes we are so miserable with our current selves and in our current state that we don't realize we've closed ourselves off to the things we hope to have in the future.

We believe we can only be truly happy when things change. We say to ourselves:

- "I'll be happy when I lose the weight."
- "I'll be happy when I make more money."
- "I'll be happy when I find love."
- "I'll be happy when I get a promotion."

But our current state of disapproval makes it difficult (if not impossible) to accomplish anything of importance—making it even more difficult to ever attain our desired state of "when."

When we don't accept who we currently are, we don't allow ourselves to enjoy the present and we miss out on a joyful life. And with all our energy focused on hating current parts of our life, we don't set ourselves up for positive change or allow our desired future to ever arrive.

Only once you decide to love yourself in your current state, you can use that power of self-love to create the destiny you desire.

In her international bestseller *You Can Heal Your Life*, Louise Hay talks a great deal about the importance of self-approval. She says, "Self-approval and self-acceptance in the now are the keys to positive changes."

She goes on to say, "I find that when we really love and accept and approve of ourselves exactly as we are, then everything in life works... Loving the self, to me, begins with never ever criticizing ourselves for anything... Remember, you have been criticizing yourself for years and it hasn't worked. Try approving of yourself and see what happens."

What you choose to think and what you choose to believe can determine your future and ultimately your levels of happiness and success.

Stop telling yourself you're not good enough; instead start being kind to yourself. Tell yourself you are wonderful, smart, attractive, loving and happy. Tell yourself that you will get that raise or promotion, that you will make more money and that you will find love.

Accepting who you are and being kind to yourself will provide an environment that will foster your future success.

Chapter Exercise:

Every morning for the next 10 days, take 10 seconds after you wake up to say the positive affirmation provided below in front of the bathroom mirror. If you want to make slight modifications, feel free to do so. But if you're struggling with what to say, use the words below.

Morning affirmation: I love the person I am. I am thankful for being alive. I am strong, I am smart, I am beautiful, and I have the power to continue to make positive changes in my life. I am in control of my destiny.

It may feel strange at first. I know that for me, it was difficult to say with a straight face the first few times. But as you continue the process, it not only gets easier, but you start to actually believe your words. And believing is the first step in making your wishes come true.

After the initial 10 days, I hope that you will notice positive results—feeling happier, more productive and more accepting of yourself. And I hope you may decide to continue the practice each morning beyond the 10-day trial period.

Your time is limited, so don't waste it living someone else's life...

– Steve Jobs

Chapter 9:
Be Your Real Self

You know who you are. You know what makes you tick and what gets you excited. But even when we know who we are and what we want, we often ignore our real selves as we strive for more—more happiness, more joy, more money, more success and more purpose. We forget about what we want and instead do what we think we should do or what others expect of us; we think that doing so will bring us more of what we want.

Stop looking for outside validation. Focus instead on internal validation. The approval or acceptance that is most important comes from within. Don't change who you are to please others. Be your true self.

Trying to be someone you're not can also be extremely taxing and rarely provides the outcome your looking for. Don't compare yourself to others; the outcome is never positive. No matter how beautiful or handsome you are, there is always someone more attractive. No matter how wealthy you are, there is always someone with more money. No matter how smart you are, there is always someone more intelligent.

You can only be truly happy when you decide to love yourself just the way you are—in this moment. That doesn't mean you can't strive to be better, but it means you need to start appreciating yourself now.

I've learned the hard way that pretending to be something you're not will never get the outcome you want. I was a business and finance major in college, and I'm not sure why, but I had my heart set on landing my dream finance job in New York City. I imagined myself working for a top Wall Street investment bank. So as graduation approached, I prepared my resume, sharpened my interview skills and got to work interviewing with Wall Street's best of the best.

It didn't take me long, though, to realize that I didn't fit in with my interviewers. I'm not sure what it was, but I sensed that my personality wasn't aligned with what they were looking for, and I started getting the feeling that the job may not be what I really wanted either. But for four years I had focused on this one outcome and wasn't ready to change course. I wasn't having great luck, so I decided to try acting more like my very conservative interviewers.

For my next scheduled interview—a big one with Wall Street giant Morgan Stanley—I wore my most conservative blue suit and white blouse and put my long blonde hair into a tight bun (something I had never done before). I even took it one step further and wore a pair of glasses, even though I had perfect vision. I kept my outgoing personality to a minimum and projected an "all business" attitude in the interview. And it worked! I got a lucrative financial analyst position in New York City.

My dream job had come to fruition. Or had it? I very quickly realized that I may have made a huge mistake. Pretending to be someone I wasn't might have landed me the job, but that position didn't fit with the real me. Sitting at a desk all day long crunching numbers and analyzing spreadsheets wasn't working.

Although my two years with Morgan Stanley proved an incredible learning experience and helped me get into a top graduate business school, I still often wonder what it would have been like had I taken a job that reflected the real me (and was not only a good fit for but also something I enjoyed). The lesson learned: Don't pretend to be something you're not; this charade will never make the real you happy.

Chapter Exercise:

Take a minute to ask yourself these three questions:

1) Are you pretending to be someone you're not?

2) Are you constantly trying to please others but forgetting what's important to you?

3) Is the real you happy?

If you're not being true to yourself, take this time to make a list of the things in your life you want to change. This acknowledgement is the first step to creating movement.

Make sure every day you do what matters most. When you know what matters most, everything makes sense. When you don't know what matters most, anything makes sense.

– Gary Keller

Chapter 10:
Do What Matters Most

I hope we can all agree that time is one of the most precious things in life. Although we don't know how long we have on this earth, we do know that it's a finite amount we can never get back—no matter how hard we may try. So the phrase "time well spent" is an important one. We can choose to waste our time or use it wisely.

There are 1,440 minutes in a day. And the one thing we can do to ensure these precious minutes are well spent? Do what matters most!

What matters most to you may encompass several areas of your life. You may categorize these priorities into a family and friends list, a health and wellness list, a work and career list and so on. But regardless of whether you have one big list that encompasses all areas of your life or several that split up the focus, you need to think long and hard about what matters most. It's important to look beyond the day, week or even year—you need to view your life as a whole.

When your time is up, you should feel like you spent it well. In her book *The Top 5 Regrets of the Dying*, Bronnie Ware recounts her time spent with the terminally ill and five common regrets she witnessed:

1) I wish I'd had the courage to live a life true to myself, not the life others expected of me

2) I wish I hadn't worked so hard

3) I wish I'd had the courage to express my feelings

4) I wish I had stayed in touch with my friends

5) I wish I had let myself be happier

After reading each of the above, ask yourself, "What can I do to ensure I don't experience this regret, too?"

I realize we are all extremely busy and daily tasks often overtake our lives and eat up valuable time. We are constantly overwhelmed, and our days can feel like they overflow with trivial tasks, unimportant conversations and unproductive activities. Because of this, it becomes even more important for us to avoid the regrets mentioned above and ask ourselves how we can:

1) Live a life true to ourselves

2) Work smarter, not harder or longer

3) Express our feelings and share our thoughts

4) Stay in touch with the people who matter most

5) Do the things that make us happy, i.e. the things that fulfill us.

Take a minute right now to reread each of the five most common regrets and ask yourself, "What can I do to ensure I don't feel the same regrets?" At the end of the chapter, we can add these items into our list of to-do's that matter.

Focusing on what's important can immensely improve our lives. How can you place your attention on only the important things and do what matters most?

Use these four steps to ensure you're focusing on what matters most:

1) Prioritize

2) Eliminate

3) Delegate

4) Schedule

Prioritize

Prioritization is key to focusing on the things that matter most. Far too many small and insignificant tasks creep into our day, causing us to waste minutes (if not hours). This wasted time prevents us from achieving the more important tasks that can truly impact our lives in positive ways.

If we can prioritize our tasks, we can free ourselves up for what matters most.

Eliminate

Not only is it important to prioritize everything on your to-do list, but it's also crucial to remove items that won't improve your life.

Many of us have overlooked items on our list collecting virtual dust. These long-standing to-do's only cause unnecessary stress. Take a good look at your inventory, and ask yourself these three questions:

1) Will this task or project improve my life?
2) Will this task or project help me achieve my end goal (one that matters)?
3) If I don't complete this task or project now, will it negatively affect my life?

Go through every item on your to-do list, and ask yourself these three questions. If you answer yes to any of them, then keep the item on your to-do list; however, if you answer no to all, remove the item from you list. If eliminating items makes you feel anxious, then file that to-do in a separate list titled: To Do Some Day In The Future.

Delegate

Once you've prioritized your list and eliminated those unimportant items that didn't add any value to your life, review the remaining items to determine whether they can be done by someone other than you. That is, see which ones you may be able to delegate to someone else. Can your spouse, sibling, friend or co-worker do this task for you? Then start delegating and free up your time for the activities that matter most.

Schedule

Research shows that people tend to do the simple, unimportant tasks first and save the more time-consuming or difficult ones for later. The issue arises since there is never enough time to get everything done, so those more important tasks never get accomplished. Consequently, we spend our days, weeks and years focused on the unimportant items on our list.

If you've done a good job prioritizing, eliminating and delegating, you should have very few (if any) unimportant items left on your list. But even so, tackle the items that matter most first to ensure you get them done. Moreover, if we do these meaningful things when we are still fresh and invigorated, we will be able to give them the focus and attention they deserve.

Try spending the first hour or two of every day working on what matters most—before checking email, social media and texts or returning any calls. Don't do anything that might distract you. Instead, focus all your attention on accomplishing your goals. You'll be amazed how one or two dedicated hours each day (which you would have spent working anyways) can be the impetus to achieving all your dreams.

In his bestselling book *Habit Stacking*, Steve Scott suggests identifying your three MITs, or Most Important Tasks. He states that focusing on your MITs before anything else "…eliminates the problem of scheduling too many activities, and the feeling of failure when you don't accomplish them all." He goes on to say, "Don't work on anything else until you have completed these MITs."

Schedule your most important tasks into your calendar just like you would an important meeting. For example, dedicate every day from 8 a.m. to 10 a.m. or 9 a.m. to 11 a.m. to what matters most, and get specific about what this means. For me, I spend my first two hours of every day writing. I know from experience that if I open my email inbox, I won't accomplish my most important to-do's, so I've made it a habit to not open any emails or answer any calls until my scheduled writing time has ended.

Time is fixed, so how do we make time for everything? You don't! The only way to make the most of the time we have and to focus on what matters most is to prioritize what needs to get done, eliminate those items that don't, delegate when we can and schedule our days.

In his bestselling book *The Purpose Driven Life*, Rick Warren says, "You become effective by being selective. It is usually meaningless work, not overwork, that wears us down, saps our strength and robs our joy." He goes on to say, "If you want your life to have impact, focus it! Stop dabbling. Stop trying to do it all. Do less."

Are you dabbling? Are you trying to do it all? Become selective and find success and joy by doing what matters most!

Chapter Exercise:

Take 15 minutes to write down everything on your to-do list. Include short- and long-term activities, projects, goals, etc. Then number each item from most important to least important.

Once you have your list, determine whether any items can be eliminated by using the three questions discussed in the chapter.

1) Will this task or project improve my life?

2) Will this task or project help me achieve my end goal (one that matters)?

3) If I don't complete this task or project now, will it negatively affect my life?

Next, determine whether anything left on the list can be delegated and set a timeframe to plan for how and when you will transition the activity. Finally, schedule the most important items into your day right now. Set aside time for the things that matter most!

Today you have two choices where forgiveness is concerned: One, continue to be angry and miserable, or two, forgive, let go, and be happy.

– Gabrielle Bernstein

Chapter 11:
Forgive Others

"Let it go!" Easier said than done, right? Is there something you can't let go of? Is there someone you haven't been able to forgive? Are you clinging to resentment? Is that bottled-up resentment making you sad or angry?

If you answered "yes" to any of these questions, it's time to learn how to forgive. Holding on to resentment will only prevent you from living a joyful life. It can even make you physically sick and miserable.

In her book *Add More-ing to Your Life*, Gabrielle Bernstein uses a waterskiing analogy to help us understand forgiveness. Having been an avid water skier growing up, I couldn't help but connect with her comparison. She tells a story of learning to ski and the wonderful feeling of getting up for the first time—floating over the water and feeling the wind in her hair and the spray on her face. But these feelings disappeared as she began to lose control. While a more seasoned water skier would simply let go of the rope, she clung on even tighter.

She says, "Once I was up, I was unwilling to let go of the rope. Even when I began to lose control, I gripped the rope tightly and tried to continue skiing. My water-skiing buddies who were watching from the boat were screaming, 'Let go of the rope!' But I didn't listen. The boat dragged me along, and even though my arms felt like they were being pulled from their sockets, I refused to let go. The waves were smacking me in the face and crashing over my head. My legs were trembling, and I felt battered and bruised. It would have been easy to blame any number of things for my predicament—the speed of the boat, my equipment, the choppiness of the water. But the truth was, I was my own obstacle that day. After succumbing to the pain in my arms, I finally let go of the rope. And once I released it, I found myself floating freely and peacefully in the water. I lay back and floated in the middle of the warm lake, fully supported by my life preserver. Happiness and relief washed over me."

I love her story because, even though holding on caused pain and undue stress, she couldn't allow herself to let go. She fought it until it was just too much. When she finally did give into the simple action of release, she discovered immediate relief. The same is true of forgiveness. Holding on causes us undue pain and suffering. Yet, although we have the power to simply let go, we often just hold on tighter, unwilling to release the rope.

Be willing to let go! Release the rope, and float freely! By forgiving, you're not just letting someone else off the hook for his or her actions, but you're freeing yourself. The moment you truly forgive, you will feel joy flood back into your body.

When you forgive, set free of all judgment linked to the situation. Too often we wait for a particular person to fail us again, meaning they most likely will. Start fresh and give the forgiven person the benefit of the doubt. Remember that holding onto anger or resentment is only hurting you.

To clarify, forgiving someone for something they did doesn't mean the action wasn't wrong. It simply means you are giving them a second chance, or a clean slate.

Forgiveness can improve your own emotional well-being. We waste far too much emotional energy resenting those around us. So let go of resentment, and allow your mind to focus on more positive parts of your life.

Many benefits come from forgiveness. In fact, the Mayo Clinic says that forgiveness can help:

- Decrease anxiety and stress
- Reduce symptoms of depression
- Strengthen the immune system
- Improve heart health
- Lower blood pressure
- Increase self-esteem

The Mayo Clinic also states that forgiveness can aid in greater spiritual and emotional well-being, something many of us strive for.

Forgiveness is the first step in allowing yourself to heal and find joy. Don't let your resentment stop you from making the most of the present. Ready to forgive? Start with these five steps:

1) Acknowledge who you want to forgive
2) Acknowledge what was done that caused you pain
3) Let go of the unhealthy obsession that comes with resentment
4) Allow yourself to stop living in the past and to make a fresh start
5) Remember that it's your choice to forgive

Although each step is important, the last one is the most critical. Understanding that it's your choice allows you to truly forgive. No one can force you to forgive. But once you realize that letting go and forgiving someone can free you, I hope you will feel inspired to do so. Forgive, let go, and move on to a better life—one that isn't consumed by anger, depression and resentment. Let go of the rope!

Chapter Exercise:

Take five to 10 minutes and review the five steps to forgiving others. Make a plan to move forward by following each step. Ask yourself, "Who do I need to forgive?" Think back on what they did to hurt you. Acknowledge the pain, and then let it go. Then find a way to tell that person you forgive them. It can be face-to-face, over the phone, in a letter or even through a text. It doesn't matter how you do it; what matters is that you let go of the anger you feel toward that person.

Make this process your resentment cleanse. Clear out all the negative thoughts associated with the person who hurt you. Cleanse your mind and move on with a clear head—one that's free of resentment and ready to experience joy.

Forgive yourself for your faults and your mistakes and move on.

– Les Brown

Chapter 12:
Forgive Yourself

We talked about the importance of forgiving others in the previous chapter, but the same goes for forgiving yourself. Just as it's healthy to forgive others for their wrongdoings and move on, you also need to learn how to let go and forgive yourself in order to start over.

Until you figure out how to forgive yourself, you won't be able to move on. When we hold onto blame for something we've done—no matter how wrong we were or how badly we acted—that guilt can become debilitating.

The only way to rid yourself of this guilt is to find self-forgiveness. I'm not suggesting you ignore what you've done, but you need to take responsibility, make things right (if you can) and then forgive yourself.

Self-forgiveness helps more than just you. When you can't forgive yourself, you not only affect your own well-being, but inevitably you also negatively impact those around you. When you're suffering from guilt, the people you love most often feel your pain.

Take theses five steps and learn how to forgive yourself.

1) Acknowledge what you've done
2) Take responsibility for your actions
3) Apologize and ask for forgiveness when appropriate
4) Make things right (if you can)
5) Let it go by replacing the guilty thought with a positive one

If you are holding onto guilt, that guilt is more than likely holding you back from being your best self and living your best life. Self-forgiveness can set you free and allow you to reach your full potential.

Forgive yourself, and land on the path to finding happiness and joy.

Chapter Exercise:

Take five to 10 minutes and review the five steps for forgiving yourself. Decide right here, right now, to free yourself and forgive. Make a plan to move forward by following each step. First, acknowledge what you did. Take responsibility for your actions, and ask for forgiveness. I know that apologizing may be difficult, but it will free you of the guilt currently weighing you down. If you can, try and make things right. Then move on by replacing your guilt with positive thoughts and actions.

Tell me and I forget. Teach me and I remember. Involve me and I learn.

– Benjamin Franklin

Chapter 13:
Learn From Others

In a previous chapter, we discussed the importance of being true to ourselves. But that doesn't mean you can't learn from others. I've found that while trying to find what makes the real me happy, surrounding myself with people I respect and admire has proven crucial to my overall success. I know we hear a great deal about the importance of finding a mentor (or mentors), and I am a believer in doing so. But I have also found that I can still learn a great deal even if someone doesn't formally commit to fulfilling that mentor title.

I've been fortunate to have several mentors throughout my career. And to be honest, I don't remember ever formally asking any of them to fill that role. In fact, over the years I simply made sure I kept in contact with these individuals, met with them on a regular basis and cultivated a professional and often personal relationship with each one.

As I moved across the country and changed careers, I did my best to continue my relationships—ultimately allowing me to create a core group of mentors I could always count on.

For the past several years, I've carried out numerous speaking engagements. No matter the size of the company or organization or the demographic of the audience, I inevitably field the question, "How do I get a mentor?" But a mentor isn't always something you officially "get;" it's often something that slowly develops over time.

In fact, sometimes the relationship evolves into more than just a mentor-mentee bond.

Just the other day, I was having lunch with one of my longtime mentors. Cathy is 10 years my senior and a very successful entrepreneur. Although Cathy and I only meet a few times a year, we've known each other for nearly a decade. Over that time, we have both built and sold multi-million dollar companies. During our most recent lunch, Cathy said something that caught me off guard. She told me how lucky she felt to have me as a mentor. What!? At first I thought I had heard incorrectly. Did *my* mentor just tell me she was happy to have me as *her* mentor?

Throughout our years of meeting and discussing business and life, I always felt as though I was getting advice from her. She was even on my company's advisory group before I sold. What I didn't realize was that—while I considered her my mentor—she also thought of me as someone who provided value to her. Her comment made me realize that the mentor-mentee relationship can evolve over time, and both parties can receive immense value from the connection.

Stop thinking of the mentor-mentee relationship as something you have to formalize. In fact, most successful people you might approach about being your mentor are so busy that they would likely decline the invitation. However, if you make your interaction less formal, the relationship often evolves, and one day you may just find yourself saying, "Thank you for being such a great mentor," to someone who never formally committed to filling that role in the first place. The best mentor-mentee relationships are those that have naturally evolved and were never forced or structured.

Remember, many unconventional opportunities that weren't previously available now exist for finding a mentor. Years ago, people didn't have the luxury of learning from other successful people unless they had written a book you could read or you had a way of connecting with them one-on-one. Today, it's much easier to learn from successful role models, as so many share their experiences though social media posts, podcasts, blogs, radio or TV interviews. Take advantage of the valuable effects these "virtual mentors" can have on your life.

If you do have the opportunity to learn firsthand from people you respect, take advantage. Make a list of three or four people you admire and respect. If it's possible to have a face-to-face connection, then make it a priority to do so. Set up a lunch or short meeting. If you're looking for advice, come prepared; if the person asks, "How can I help you?" make sure you have a good answer—one that is short and succinctly gets your point across.

When I launched my first magazine, I read books and periodicals discussing the industry, watched numerous online interviews and met with as many experts as were willing to give me their time. But I also learned from many people who I never met in person. These virtual mentors provided just as much invaluable advice as a face-to-face mentor would have.

If an in-person meet-up isn't a possibility, find the best way to learn from that individual (or individuals). Does she or he have a podcast or blog? Do they hold live webinars? Have they written a book or do they write articles for popular magazines or websites? Knowledge from experts today is amazingly easy to access and extremely valuable, too. Take advantage of these virtual mentors.

Chapter Exercise:

Make a list of three people you'd like to learn from in a face-to-face environment. Call or email them now and set up a time to grab coffee or lunch. Also make a list of three people you admire, but most likely can't meet face-to-face. Find a way to connect with them. Follow them on social media or read their blog or book. Schedule time in your calendar to connect. For example, I schedule time to listen to a few people's podcasts. Although they aren't formal mentors and most likely don't even know I exist, I get a great deal out of this virtual mentor relationship.

FAITH

Infinite striving to be the best is man's duty; it is its own reward. Everything else is in God's hands.

– Mahatma Gandhi

Chapter 14:
Have Faith

I didn't grow up in a religious household. My father is Jewish, and my mother Catholic. At first, neither of their families were happy with the union. And in order to not ruffle any more feathers, my parents decided to not impose either of their religious beliefs on us kids. In fact, we didn't practice religion at all. But as I grew up and found my way to God, I realized that—even though my parents kept their beliefs to themselves—all the life lessons they taught my sister and me could easily have come straight out of the scriptures.

I learned on my own (and in my own time) to have faith in God, but my dad was the one who taught me to have faith in myself. I quickly discovered that these two things—faith in a higher power and faith in oneself—go hand in hand when looking for purpose and striving toward success.

I truly believe that God put us on this Earth to achieve great things and to live a joyful and compassionate life, but I also believe God leaves the actions—the "how" we live—up to us. No matter what religion we practice or whether we practice at all, we have the power to determine how we exist—with good or evil, with passion or apathy, with joy or sorrow, with greed or compassion, with love or hatred. We must find our own joy and happiness, and we must put forth the effort needed to make things happen. We have the power of choice. It's up to us to move forward in a direction that matters.

Rick Warren, the author of *A Purpose Driven Life,* said in a TED Talk, "There are three levels of living—the survival level of living, the success level of living and the significance level of living… it comes down to why am I here, what am I here for and where am I going." Your faith, whether in a higher power, in yourself or in both, can take you from survival mode to success and ultimately lead you toward a life of significance.

Your faith determines everything—your level of joy, your strength of relationships, your degree of confidence, your measure of success and ultimately how you live your life.

I know faith is very personal, and I've probably already said more than I should (and perhaps even offended some in the process). However, although I do think it's important to share my personal views and beliefs, this chapter mainly focuses on having faith not solely in God or a higher power but also in oneself, as a way to achieve joy and success and to truly live the life you desire.

Having faith in yourself is similar to believing in yourself, but it takes the process one step further. It's not only about being convinced you can achieve something; it means having faith that if you put in the work, great things will come. It's about letting down your guard and allowing the Universe to give you what you deserve. It's about opening your mind and soul and being willing to receive any good that comes your way. Too often we close ourselves off, thinking that good fortune is not ours to have. When we block ourselves from receiving those gifts, though, we miss out on unbelievable opportunities.

Having faith can transform your life. Focusing on the good, even in—*especially* in—seemingly negative situations, can allow positive events to flow your way.

Have faith in your ability to make positive change in your own life and in the lives of others. Decide to love yourself just how you are right now—faults and all. That doesn't mean you can't strive to be better; it just means you need to start appreciating who you already are in this moment. This acceptance marks the first step of having faith, and it ultimately makes positive change possible.

I've discovered that having faith comes more easily when I find time for quiet. There is so much noise in the world. With social media distractions, political talk, TV shows and so on, there's more clamor than ever before. All this commotion can make it difficult to slow down and take stock in who we are, what we want and, most importantly, how we plan to get where we want to go.

Simply being still can offer the best way to move forward. Make it a priority to find a minimum of 10 minutes of quiet each day. If this seems overwhelming or impossible (as it did for me in the beginning), start gradually and build your way up. Allow yourself three or four minutes every morning (or evening) to sit still and shut out all the noise.

During this time, be thankful for what you have—no matter how minimal it may seem. Simply changing your attitude can open you up to all the marvelous possibilities coming your way.

In chapter 5, I shared how to start a meditation practice. If you're new to meditation, review the steps and start today. During your quiet time or meditation, open up your mind, have faith in yourself and in those around you, and allow good fortune to enter your life.

Chapter Exercise:

Take a few minutes every day to quiet your mind and be thankful for what you have right now. If possible, try to schedule this tranquil time—no matter how brief—for the same time each day. This will help you develop a daily habit of taking the time to quiet your mind, be thankful and open yourself to the possibility of good fortune.

He who is not courageous enough to take risks will accomplish nothing in life.

– Muhammad Ali

Chapter 15:
Let Go of Fear and Doubt

Don't let fear and doubt hold you back. Fear can so easily derail your opportunities for success. Overcoming our fears and learning to take risks can open doors to unlimited possibilities and help you realize your ultimate potential.

The first step involves being aware of your fears, acknowledging them and drilling down into the worst-case scenario possible. Often our fear and the potential outcome causing that fear don't match up. That is, our level of fear far outweighs what we're scared of. What's the worst thing that can happen?

Now if you're talking about climbing Mount Everest during a bad storm, your fears are likely warranted. But if your fear is keeping you from speaking at an industry conference, your fear factor probably outweighs any potential negative outcome. What's the worst that can happen? Even if you don't do a stellar job, you'll most likely learn from the experience and know how to do a better job next time.

You need to connect your fear to the potential negative outcome and then put your fear into perspective.

Every single time I've been scared to do something but did it anyway, I either learned something amazing or moved my career forward.

In 2005, for example, I had the great pleasure of meeting Mark Burnett, the creator and producer of some of the most watched reality shows in history including *Survivor*, *The Voice* and *The Apprentice*. The truth is, I almost missed the opportunity. In fact, my fears nearly kept me from an incredible and life-changing experience.

In 2004 a good friend of mine from graduate school, Kelly Perdew, won the second season of *The Apprentice: Donald Trump*. Shortly after his victory and the start of his new job with Trump, he called me to report what a blast he was having in New York City. But more than that, he wanted to encourage me to try out for the next season. Kelly and I had been on many project teams together during grad school, and he explained how his experience on the reality show was very similar—you get thrown into a group of individuals you hardly know and are expected to work together to achieve an end goal. Knowing my work style, Kelly thought I would thrive in *The Apprentice*'s environment.

At the time of this first call, I had just left a high-paying job as chief marketing officer for a $700-million company and for the first time in my life was trying to make it as an entrepreneur. In fact, I had just launched a national running magazine and hired my first two employees.

I explained to Kelly that all my efforts needed to be focused on making my new venture a successful one. I also explained to Kelly that I had no interest in real estate and that the first two seasons of *The Apprentice* had focused heavily on real estate challenges, with the winner receiving a position in the Trump organization that focused on real estate projects.

But Kelly didn't take my "no thank you, I'm not interested" to heart. I'm not exaggerating when I say that he called me every few days for nearly a month. It finally got to the point where I'd see his caller ID on my phone and ignore it.

It may sound as if Kelly finally wore me down with his consistent phone calls; in reality, during one of Kelly's final calls, he informed me that Martha Stewart was going to host the next installment of *The Apprentice*. When I heard the news, I no longer had the "I'm not interested in real estate" excuse. In fact, Kelly knew I was a huge Martha fan. And having just launched a national magazine, I had something in common with her (although my magazine was much smaller than *Martha Stewart Living*), and I became more interested than ever before.

But how could I leave my company while it was in its infancy? On the morning of the mass open casting call, I almost skipped the interview. What was holding me back? Fear! I'd like to believe that the only reason I was having second thoughts stemmed from the fear of leaving my business for nine weeks of filming. But in truth, it was more than that. I was fearful that I might fail, I was fearful that I might make a fool of myself on national TV, and I was fearful that my shy personality wouldn't mesh well with a reality show.

But while my fears were strong, I eventually looked past them and saw the opportunity for what it really was— potential for a life-altering experience.

The first interview seemed insignificant but led to a series of follow-up interviews that eventually led to a final week-long interview in Los Angeles. At this final stage, 50 men and women were vying for 16 available cast slots. Although my fears were still present, I no longer let them hold me back.

I still remember the week like it was yesterday. We were all sequestered to our individual rooms and were only allowed to leave when we were requested for an interview or test. About halfway through the week, we had our first large group interview with Mark Burnett and several of his producers. All the candidates were lined up by gender outside the hotel conference room. When it was my group's turn to enter, I was first in line. As we entered the room, we saw 10 chairs lined up in a long row, all facing Mark and his team.

Having been first in line, I ended up being seated in the farthest seat from the door, followed by nine well-dressed women. Mark made a short introduction for himself and his team and then requested that each of us take 60 seconds to introduce ourselves. I mentioned my finance and marketing background and that I had just left a chief marketing officer position of a large corporation to launch a national magazine. With the exception of one lawyer in the group, the other eight women all had extremely creative jobs—chef, glassblower, fashion designer, caterer, etc. In fact, the lawyer and I were the only corporate types in the group.

After the brief introductions, Mark asked the group who we thought would be the least likely candidate to win *The Apprentice* based on the short introductions. Starting with the person farthest from me, each uttered my name until all nine had declared that I would be the least likely to win. I can still hear each of the women in the room saying my name one after the other—"Dawna, Dawna, Dawna…"

When Mark finally got to me, instead of asking for my answer, he asked me how the unanimous response made me feel. I reiterated a question I had asked several times during my weeks of interviewing. I asked if Martha was seeking another domestic diva like herself or if she was looking for someone to help run her company. Mark confirmed what I had heard repeatedly throughout the interview process: Martha was looking for someone to help grow her business, not someone who could craft, cook or decorate.

I then asked Mark if he would allow me to pose a question to the group, and I was surprised when he agreed. So I turned to the group and asked if anyone could tell me last year's revenues for Martha Stewart Living Omnimedia. Not one person said a peep. I turned to Mark and asked if I could ask one more question, and he once again agreed. I then told the group that the revenues were either just over 3 million, just over 30 million or just over 300 million. But once again, no one dared to take a guess. I then turned to Mark and his team, saying that I'd like to answer his original question. I then commented, "Not one of the nine people in the room competing against me would win."

With that, the crew smirked and we were led out of the interview and back to our rooms. I immediately phoned my husband and announced I was pretty confident I would get on the show! As fear once again crept in, I had to work hard to push it out of my mind and focus only on the amazing opportunity that might be coming my way.

For those of you who don't know me, you may think I sound rather bold and extremely self-confident to have stood up for myself in the group interview. Truthfully, I'm rather shy until I get to know people. To this day, I believe that the spectacular situation of having everyone unanimously pick me provided controversy that the production team liked—helping me secure my spot on the show.

To make a very long story a little shorter, I was chosen as one of the 16 candidates and, after nine weeks of filming, I emerged the winner of Martha's *Apprentice*. I spent the next year in New York working closely with Martha and commuting back to Florida on a weekly basis to ensure my own magazine was running smoothly.

To say the experience was worthwhile would be an understatement. I not only became vice president of business development—a title Martha and I came up with after she learned more about my corporate experience—but she gave me the opportunity to learn about many aspect of her business. I wrote a regular column in her magazine, appeared regularly on her nationally televised show *MARTHA* and worked on many special projects during my apprenticeship. It was a year of many "firsts" for me, and the experience truly altered my life. And to think that I almost let fear hold me back from attending that first interview!

Don't let unfounded fears hold you back from opportunities that can impact your life in a positive way. Don't let your fears rob you of an incredible experience that could catapult your career or simply bring joy to your life.

Chapter Exercise:

Spend a few minutes and determine whether fear is holding you back. If so, ask yourself, "What's the worse thing that can happen?" Then go after your dreams!

Be thankful for what you have; you'll end up having more. If you concentrate on what you don't have, you will never, ever have enough.

– Oprah Winfrey

Chapter 16:
Give Thanks

O f all the tips for improving one's life, I've found this one to have the quickest impact. It takes only minutes, if not seconds, to incorporate into your life. This single, super-simple act has made all the difference for me.

Let me explain. This past year, I was baptized and confirmed and became a Christian. In doing so, we were asked during one of our Right of Christian Initiation of Adults (RCIA) meetings to think about what to give up during Lent .

I know it's common for people to give up chocolate, alcohol or sugar and, although I did do this (I gave up chocolate), I decided to also add something into my life during that period. So just as I gave up chocolate, I added in a morning prayer of gratitude and thanks.

It started out as something I planned to practice only during Lent, but it made such a dramatic and noticeable difference in my day, that I have continued to do this simple task every morning before getting out of bed. It takes only a couple minutes, but its effect is enormous.

Throughout this book, I share many tips and provide several tools to help you find more joy and more meaning in your life—tools that will help you capture the life you want and deserve. But, if you do just one thing, I urge you to make this morning prayer part of your daily routine. I'm confident you'll be amazed by how such a small act can have such an extremely powerful ability to change your outlook on life. It has truly made a huge difference in my life, and I know it can make a difference for you, too.

Although I address my prayer to God, it doesn't have to be a religious prayer. Do what works for you. If you simply want to thank the Universe for giving you another day on Earth, then do so. If you want to make a promise to yourself to try and live your best life that day, then do so. Do what makes sense for you. Just make sure you focus on being thankful for the gift of life. Then get out of bed, harness your power, and make those small shifts you're learning in this book; I guarantee you will be on your way to living a life you desire.

Chapter Exercise:

When you wake up tomorrow morning, before you even get out of bed, take a few minutes to say a little prayer of thanks. Try doing this for the next five to seven days, and see if it makes a difference. I'm confident it will.

FRIENDS & FAMILY

Family is not an important thing.
It's everything.

– Michael J. Fox

Chapter 17:
Put Family First

Have you ever heard an older person or someone on their deathbed say, "I wish I would have spent *less* time with the people I love most?" Of course not. As we get older, the things that matter most are the ones we love the most, the memories we created with them and the legacy we leave behind.

For so many of us, we're too busy in our day-to-day lives to envision the big picture. Family often takes a backseat to work and other obligations. We assume that, since it's family, these people will always be around later. But what if later comes too soon?

I have a very good friend who lost his teenage son. I think about his misfortunate often. How he can cope and still be a positive and fun-to-be-around person is beyond me. I know he struggled for years to accept his loss, but I also know from talking with him that he made the most of the time he did have with his son. He had no idea he would lose a child, but he built a strong relationship with his son and spent a great deal of quality time with him. I'm sure it didn't make losing his son any easier, but at least he knows that he made the most of every minute they did have together.

Most of us can't say the same about our children. We think that we can do more with them tomorrow or next week—assuming that time will come. Don't assume anything. Put your family first right now—while you can. Make amazing memories before it's too late.

It's important to recognize the people who matter most in your life and to spend quality time with them now. Be available for important events and don't take for granted how much your presence means. You may not think it's crucial for you to attend your son or daughters' second-grade sing-along, but remember that you'll never have another chance to experience that event. Spend time with the people who matter to you—your spouse, significant other, siblings, parents, sons and/or daughters, etc.

I realize you may not be able to make every special family event or function, but choose wisely and let family take center stage in your life. My kids know that I work full-time and that I can't always be at every school function, but they also know I do everything I can to attend all the important ones. I know how much it means to them to have me there, and I also know that these events bring joy to my life.

As you put more energy into those individuals who are most important to you, also remember one of the greatest gifts you can give to another person is simply saying, "I love you!" If you love someone, tell him or her now, and tell him or her often. Not only will it make them feel great, but it will make *you* feel great.

Chapter Exercise:

Take a few minutes and tell three people today how special they are. You'll be amazed at how this very quick and simple act can brighten up their day and at the same time bring you more joy.

I used to think that the worst thing in life was to end up alone. It's not. The worst thing in life is to end up with people who make you feel alone.

– Robin Williams

Chapter 18:
Surround Yourself With Positive People

For the past 10-plus years, I've delivered motivational talks and keynotes all over the country. With only a few exceptions, I always begin them with a simple exercise. I ask the audience members to raise a hand if they've had a difficult few days or weeks or even month or year. I always have a few people who are brave enough to raise a hand.

I promise not to ask any details as I pick one person to stand up and walk over to the stage. For the sake of this example, let's call the woman selected from the audience "Jane." I then ask the audience to do me a favor. When Jane walks up to the stage, approaches the microphone and introduces herself with a simple, "Hi, I'm Jane," I ask that the entire room to stand up and hoot, cheer, clap or do anything that shows their excitement and enthusiasm for Jane.

An interesting thing always happens when I perform this little experiment. Jane feels better, the audience is more energized, and I just proved the first lesson in my talk: Positive energy is contagious.

You may have heard of the law of attraction—the ability of positive thought to bring positive results to your life. The same rings true with people. Negative people can bring negative vibes into your life, while positive people bring uplifting and positive vibes.

As individuals we constantly send out thoughts and emotions that bring back what we put out. That is, positive energy attracts positive energy and negative energy attracts negative energy. So not only do you want to bestow your positive energy on others, but you want to surround yourself with people who are doing the same.

In her worldwide bestseller *The Secret*, Rhonda Byrne deems the law of attraction to be the great secret of life. She says, "Thoughts are magnetic, and thoughts have a frequency. As you think thoughts, they are sent out into the Universe, and they magnetically attract all like things that are on the same frequency. Everything sent out returns to the source—you."

If you are the source, doesn't it make sense that—just as positive thoughts attract positive outcomes—surrounding yourself with positive people will help you attract even more positive energy? And when you fill your mind with positive thoughts and your environment with positive people, you can take advantage of all the amazing opportunities that present themselves.

Chapter Exercise:

Think of the most positive people you know and find a way to spend more time with them. Meet for lunch, or schedule a morning coffee break or happy hour. If this person doesn't live nearby, take the time to connect over the phone or video chat. Reach out today, and make it happen.

In learning you will teach,
and in teaching you will learn.

– Phil Collins

Chapter 19:
Become a Passionate Teacher

I had lunch the other day with a good friend. She recently sold her company and was in the process of building another one. Although she was extremely busy with her new endeavor, she seemed happy and in a good place to embark on her next journey.

During lunch, she began to talk about how helping other entrepreneurs and especially female entrepreneurs gives her great pride. The conversation made me realize that teaching others can be just as rewarding as learning from others. If you have a skill to share, think about becoming a passionate teacher to others.

You may be thinking, "I don't have time to be a mentor, " but teaching others can come in many forms. It doesn't have to be the time-consuming one-on-one coaching we often think of when we hear the word "mentoring." Just as I mentioned the many ways to find virtual mentors, countless ways exist to share your knowledge and passion with others without investing huge amounts of time.

Part of leading a life of purpose—one full of passion and joy—involves utilizing your skills to help others. This could be as intensive as mentoring a group of men or women on a weekly or monthly basis or as simple as sharing your knowledge on a blog or through a book or podcast.

Find what might work best for you, and give it a try. You may be surprised just how much you get out of sharing your skills and knowledge with others.

In the past, I've done one-on-one mentoring. I've helped my mentees flourish in the workplace, get promoted, get into college, follow their passions and even switch careers. But this one-on-one mentoring can be extremely time-consuming, so as my schedule became more over-extended, I found alternative solutions.

More recently, I've been sharing my knowledge via blog posts, videos, newsletters, guest posts, and my books and online courses. This allows me to continue to share and help others, but I get the added benefit of reaching and hopefully helping even more people in less time.

If you have a passion or skill you want to share, why not think about writing a book, starting a podcast or simply guest posting on popular blogs? If you want to write a book, I share a simple-to-follow plan in my book *Book Accelerator: How to Write a Bestseller in 16 Weeks—Boost Your Business, Increase Your Income and Get Noticed.* You can find out more at BookAccelerator.com. Also, if you've dreamed of landing a book deal and working with a traditional publisher, check out my free ebook: *How to Write a Book Proposal That Sells!: 15 Secrets to Earning Six Figures for Your Book.* Get your free copy at BookAccelerator.com

Writing a book is one of the most rewarding things I've ever done. Publishing my first book changed my life for the better. It catapulted my income, opened countless doors, landed me five-figure speaking engagements and a six-figure traditional book deal, in addition to getting me regular appearances on TV and radio shows as an expert guest.

I believe that anyone who wants to write a book, feels passionate about a specific topic or has expertise worth sharing, should publish. If you have a skill or passion that can help others, I urge you to share it. There are many ways to pass on your knowledge. Find the one that works best for you.

Chapter Exercise:

If you have the time, make it a priority to mentor a few individuals. If time is too tight, try finding alternative ways to reach out and help people learn from you. And don't forget about the unique opportunities that may exist in your community. Membership clubs, entrepreneurial organizations, schools and so on always have a need for expert advice. Share your knowledge however you can. Not only will others reap the benefits of learning from you, but you will also be amazed at how much you get out of helping others. It's truly a win-win!

IT'S NOT TOO LATE

Take care of your body.
It's the only place you have to live.

– Jim Rohn

Chapter 20:
Take Care of Yourself

I'd be remiss if I didn't mention personal health as part of leading a better life. As we all know, our health plays into our overall happiness. However, when we're healthy, we often take for granted the importance of taking care of our bodies and ourselves.

Like many, I am a fan of motivational guru Tony Robbins. But the reason I'm such a huge fan isn't just because he has the power to help transform people's lives by getting them to believe in themselves and take action, but also because he constantly stresses the importance of taking care of our bodies. In fact, he says, "The more efficient your body, the better you feel and the more you will use your talent to produce outstanding results." Tony realizes that taking care of yourself and your body is an important aspect of achieving a life of success, purpose and joy.

My healthy living philosophy is very similar; it centers on eating clean and staying active as a base for everything else. I try to move every day whether that means running, biking, walking or simply playing with my kids. I think focusing on my health makes me better at everything I do. Being healthy isn't about doing the right thing 100% of the time; it's about doing the right thing most of the time. If I slip up, I just move forward and don't let it derail my good intentions.

I look at even the smallest of accomplishments as a good start, like running five minutes longer, walking an extra mile, making it to three yoga classes rather than the normal two, taking 10 minutes a day to meditate or choosing a healthy snack over an unhealthy one. I realize that even small shifts contribute to helping me live a better, healthier life. Small shifts can help ensure you're making your health a priority and that you will be around to enjoy the fruits of your labor. Focus on these four key areas for better health and well-being.

1) Healthy Eating
2) Exercise
3) Hydration
4) Sleep

Let's take a look at each area and see how you can begin to make small changes that will have big results. And remember, it's never too late to start taking better care of yourself.

Healthy Eating

Several years ago on my radio program, I welcomed natural food chef Alex Jamieson as a guest. At the time, Alex was married to Morgan Spurlock, the director and star of the Academy Award-nominated documentary *Super Size Me*. In the film, Spurlock restricted his diet to three McDonald's™ meals a day for 30 days. To compound things, he also created a rule that he had to "super size" his meals anytime a server asked.

Not surprisingly, Spurlock had gained 24.5 pounds by the experiment's end. Yet beyond the weight gain, the lack of nutrients present in his McDonald's™-only diet severely damaged Spurlock's body. On the twenty-first day, he suffered heart palpitations, and his internist strongly urged that he quit. Alex confessed that both his energy and sex drive waned during the experiment. He also watched his cholesterol rise 65 points and he suffered from massive cravings, headaches and liver issues.

In response to this film, many viewers got caught up in the number of calories Spurlock consumed and his consequential weight gain (almost a pound a day!). I'll admit that I, too, found the weight increase unbelievable, yet I was more struck by the damaging effects of the high-saturated fat, nutrient-deficient diet on Spurlock's overall health. By eating highly-processed foods, you deprive your body of the nutrients needed to survive and thrive. While Spurlock's diet gives an extreme example, it wasn't that far removed from the Standard American Diet (SAD).

Are you giving your body what it needs to thrive?

Focus on eliminating fast food and pre-packaged convenience food from your diet. In their place, swap in wholesome options like fruits, vegetables and whole grains. I realize that eating healthy can take more time and effort, but planning ahead can help ensure your success. Keep healthy snacks on hand so that the next time you get too busy to do anything but visit the drive-through, you'll have easy access to some healthy alternatives to get you through the day.

Exercise

Make exercise a priority; even better, make it a habit. A Duke University study found that more than 40% of the decisions we make on a daily basis aren't decisions at all; rather, they are habits. It has been shown that changing just one habit can be the catalyst for changing many. For example, curtailing late-night snacking may help you go to bed earlier, wake up feeling refreshed, prompt exercise first thing in the morning and inspire a healthier breakfast following your workout.

If changing just one habit can lead to other positive changes, adjusting bad habits becomes very appealing. Luckily, it's possible to break detrimental habits and replace them with better ones. But how do you take the first step?

In his *New York Times* bestselling book *The Power of Habit*, Pulitzer Prize-winning investigative reporter Charles Duhigg explains that habits become routines by first presenting a trigger or cue, which is then followed by a routine and finally a reward. The cue-routine-reward cycle, or the "Habit Loop" as Duhigg calls it, will form a habit if repeated over and over. Eventually the cue alone can cause a craving. For example, if you always eat a candy bar at 3:30 p.m., studies show you'll most likely start craving a candy bar at that time each day. Simply seeing the clock hit 3:30 (the cue) is all your body needs to ignite the craving.

Understanding the habit loop can help you change your habits. Do you know the cues and rewards associated with your unhealthy patterns?

You can use Duhigg's equation to not only change bad habits into good ones, but also to create an entirely new habit. For example, if you want to start exercising first thing in the morning, try setting out your workout clothes in a highly visible place in your room or bathroom before you go to bed each night (your new cue). For the next week, as soon as you get up, go to the bathroom and brush you teeth, put on your workout clothes, and go for a walk or run or head to the gym or an exercise/yoga class. It doesn't matter the type of exercise you pursue, just get started as soon as you don your workout clothes (new routine). When you finish your workout, come home and place a star or check mark on your calendar or a congratulatory "Good job today!" in your electronic calendar (reward). You will be amazed how following this simple equation can quickly build a new habit.

Remember, changing a habit IS possible. All you need to do is identify the cue, routine and reward. Keep the cue and reward constant, and simply insert a new, healthier routine into the equation. Over time, that new pattern will become a habit—one that can help you take better care of yourself.

Hydration

Staying well hydrated can enhance mental clarity, slow the aging process, improve digestion, relieve joint pain and help eliminate toxins. The best news? It takes minimal effort. Try keeping a bottle of water with you at all times—in your purse or briefcase, on your desk or in your car. If you're not fond of the taste (or lack thereof), try flavoring it with a splash of fresh fruit juice, or find a no-calorie or low-calorie flavored water that you enjoy. Just make sure you read labels to avoid any brands that contain excess sugar or artificial sweeteners. It goes without saying, the more you enjoy the taste of your water, the more likely you will be to drink it. This may sound a little extreme, but setting a reminder on your computer or cell phone can also help keep you on top of sipping throughout the day.

Sleep

Try going to bed just 15 minutes earlier each night until you regularly retire at a decent hour; also, aim for seven to eight hours of sleep per night. If you have trouble falling asleep, try doing some light stretching or meditation before bedtime, or take a warm bath and drink a cup of soothing, naturally-decaffeinated tea like chamomile. Getting adequate sleep brings many health benefits including improved memory, decreased stress, heightened creativity, improved athletic performance and reduced anxiety and depression. Simply going to bed early can help you take better care of yourself.

It's difficult—if not impossible—to have a joy-filled life when you are in poor health or, even worse, in pain. Like every other step discussed in the book, you have control over this aspect of your life. You have the option of either treating your body well or abusing it. But getting or staying healthy won't happen automatically. You need to take action and make a conscious decision to prioritize your health. No matter where you currently fall on the health spectrum, it's never too late to make lifestyle adjustments that can improve your overall well-being.

When I was younger and an avid athlete, it never dawned on me to question why my parents didn't exercise. As a kid, I assumed that once you got older, you only went to work, spent time with your family and didn't have time for much else.

Back then I was involved in sports because I loved it, not because anyone forced me or because I knew it was good for me. In fact, it probably wasn't until my early 20s, when I no longer had organized sports to keep me active, that I realized the importance of exercise to my overall health (and waistline).

I became an avid gym goer and runner (and later triathlete) in my 20s and 30s, and I became very vocal about the benefits of exercise. But no matter how hard I tried, I could never convince my parents to partake.

I know now that most of my dad's illnesses—heart disease, high blood pressure, diabetes and chronic obstruction pulmonary disease or COPD—are preventable diseases that may have been avoided had he exercised and eaten more healthfully.

My dad, now in his mid 70s, never watched his diet and never exercised as an adult. And when I compare my dad to my friends' more active dads of similar ages, the contrast is unbelievable. Those who remained active throughout their lives and still exercise regularly are now in far better health and able to enjoy their golden years.

I wish I had encouraged my dad to exercise when he still could. I wish I had pushed him to make his health a priority. I have made exercise and eating healthy a priority in my life, and I hope you will, too.

Chapter Exercise:

Determine right now how you can make small shifts in four key areas—healthy eating, exercise, hydration and sleep. Start with small changes and build upon them. Pack a healthy snack and carry it with you wherever you go. When hunger strikes, you'll be more likely to make a good choice. Try setting aside 20 minutes to go for a walk, or add five more minutes to your current exercise routine. Start your morning with 24 ounces of water. This will jump-start your water intake and help you reach your daily goal. And lastly, try going to bed 15 minutes earlier today. Continue to add an additional 15 minutes of sleep each night, until you reach a minimum of seven to eight hours. I realize this is a lot to digest at once, but remember that these small shifts take very little time or effort and yield big results! Give them a try.

The fear of death follows from the fear of life. A man who lives fully is prepared to die at any time.

– Mark Twain

Chapter 21:
Live Every Day Like
It's Your Last

L ife moves quickly, and if we don't make a conscious effort to build the life we want and deserve, it will simply pass us by. Then we'll never experience the wonderful life we are meant to live—one full of happiness, security, passion, significance and purpose.

Start living the life you want right now! The life you desire is within reach; you just have to grab it and truly want it. And I mean *really* want it. Wake up ready to seize the day. Say aloud or in your head, "Today is going to be a great day!", "I'm excited to see where today takes me," or even a simple, "Let's do this!"

And remember, it's never too late to get the life you desire. Age doesn't matter when it comes to finding a life of purpose and joy. In fact, so many people don't find their true calling until much later in life.

Martha Stewart didn't write her first book *Entertaining* until she was 41! That book launched her career as a domestic diva, and her highly successful Martha Stewart Living Omnimedia company followed.

Tim and Nina Zagat didn't launch their restaurant review guide until both were 51. Vera Wang was 40 when she decided to become a fashion designer, and Julia Child made her television debut at age 51.

Laura Ingalls Wilder wrote the first *Little House* book at age 65, which later evolved into the popular TV show *Little House on the Prairie*. Duncan Hines was 73 when he licensed his name to a company that developed cake mixes; we all know how that turned out. Success can happen at any age.

In her international bestseller *You Can Heal Your Life*, Louise Hay recounts a story about one of her clients, a 79-year-old singing teacher. Louise says, "...several of her [client's] students were making television commercials. She wanted to do this too, but was afraid." She goes on to say, "I supported her totally and explained, 'There is nobody like you. Just be yourself. Do it for the fun of it. There are people out there looking for exactly what you have to offer. Let them know you exist.'" So her client did as she instructed and contacted several casting directors. Almost immediately, the 79-year-old singing teacher had gigs working on commercials, TV and in magazines—just more proof that it's never too late to go after what you want.

If you knew you only had a finite amount of time left, would you go after what you want? Are you willing to take action? Are you willing to let go of fear, limiting beliefs and negative self-talk? If you can answer "yes" to any of these, then you're ready to move toward a better life.

Make a conscious decision right now to open yourself up to the life you deserve. Don't wait until a future date to do the things that matter most. Take what you learned throughout this book and:

- Believe in yourself
- Go after success rather than waiting for it to find you
- Visualize your success
- Be all in
- Slow down to speed up
- Never give up
- See life as a gift
- Practice self-acceptance

- Be your real self
- Do what matters most
- Forgive others
- Forgive yourself
- Learn from others
- Have faith
- Let go of fear and worry
- Give thanks for what you have
- Put family first
- Surround yourself with positive people
- Become a passionate teacher
- Take care of yourself
- Live every day like it's your last

You have the power to live the life you desire. Don't wait! Begin to make the small shifts that can forever change your life for the better. A life full of significance, joy and meaning awaits. Use the lessons and exercises you learned in this book, and go get it!

Chapter Exercise:

Make a conscious decision RIGHT NOW to open yourself up to the life you deserve.

Appendix I:
A Better Life Recap

You Can Have a Better Life covers a great deal of information, and I realize it might be a lot to digest at once. I've developed this quick summation to help you follow through on each of the 21 steps that will help you lead a life of significance, joy and purpose—ultimately achieving all your goals and dreams. Use the recap as an easy-to-use, step-by-step guide.

Believe in yourself

Don't let your current beliefs hold you back. The first step to finding success is to believe you are capable of having it. Most of us want more success, but few of us actually believe we are worthy or that we have what it takes. Wanting and believing must work in tandem in order for us to find success. Put aside all your fears, all your negative thoughts and all your beliefs of unworthiness. You are worthy of success.

Don't wait for success to find you

Positive change only comes with action. If you push ahead, the effort you put forth will begin that forward motion needed to capture success. Success isn't going to find you just because you want it to. It's not going to seek you out simply because you're a good person. It's going to happen when you desire it, deserve it and most importantly act upon it.

Visualize your success

Thoughts are more powerful than you think. Our thoughts can determine our reality. If we can learn to control our thoughts, we have the ability to create our own reality.

Slow down to speed up

It can be difficult to find clarity and purpose with so many thoughts running through your head and so many items lining your to-do list. Sometimes the answer to our problems lie right in front of us; we're just moving too quickly to get a good glimpse of them. The ability to slow down and analyze your actions may be all you need to finally achieve success.

Be all in

The one thing successful, happy people have in common? They are "all in." It doesn't matter what they are doing, these folks do it with a notable and admirable passion. Are you doing everything in your power to move yourself to a place of joy and abundance? In order to succeed, you need to be "all in." Success is waiting for you. Give it everything you have, and go get it!

Never give up

Most successful people fail over and over before finally succeeding. The thing that sets them apart is that they don't give up. They learn from their failures, make adjustments and try again. Take risks, stumble, and get back up. Learn from mistakes and do it again, until you no longer stumble and instead leap forward and thrive! Success awaits just around the corner.

See life as a gift

Take a second to step back and realize how lucky you are. Make a personal commitment to view life as a gift. Find more joy in your life, just as it exists today. That doesn't mean you can't strive for more, but appreciate the life you currently have.

Practice self-acceptance

Stop telling yourself you're not good enough; instead, start being kind to yourself. Believe that you are wonderful, smart, attractive, loving and happy. Tell yourself that you will get that raise or promotion, you will make more money, and you will find love.

Accepting who you are and being kind to yourself will provide an environment that will foster your future success.

Be your real self

Stop looking for outside validation, and instead focus on internal validation. The approval or acceptance that is most important comes from you, not from others. Don't change who you are to please others. Trying to be someone you're not can be extremely taxing and rarely provides the outcome you're looking for.

Do what matters most

The only way to make the most of the time we have and to focus on what matters most is to prioritize what needs to get done, eliminate those items that don't, delegate when we can and schedule our day. There are 1,440 minutes in a day and one thing can ensure these minutes are well spent: Do what truly matters!

Forgive others

Holding on to resentment will only keep you from living a joyful life. It can even make you physically sick and miserable. The moment you truly forgive, you will feel joy flood back into your body. Forgive, let go, and move on to secure a better life—one that isn't consumed by anger, depression and resentment.

Forgive yourself

When we hold onto blame for something we've done—no matter how wrong we were or how badly we acted—that guilt can become debilitating. The only way to rid yourself of this guilt is to find self-forgiveness. Self-forgiveness can set you free and allow you to reach your full potential. Forgive yourself, and land on the path to finding happiness and joy.

Learn from others

Surround yourself with people you respect. Learning from others can be a crucial part of your future success. If you have the opportunity to learn face-to-face from someone you admire, take advantage of it. But remember, learning from others can come in many forms. It's easier today than ever before to utilize technology for finding virtual mentors who can help you on your path to success.

Have faith

No matter what religion we practice or whether we practice at all, we have the power to determine how we exist—with good or evil, with passion or apathy, with joy or sorrow, with greed or compassion, with love or hatred. We must find our own happiness, and we must put forth the effort needed to make things happen. We have the power of choice. It's up to us to move forward in a direction that matters. Your faith determines everything—your level of joy, your strength of relationships, your degree of confidence, your measure of success and ultimately how you live your life.

Let go of fear and worry

Don't let fear and doubts hold you back. Fear can so easily derail your opportunities for success. Overcoming our fears and learning to take risks opens doors to unlimited possibilities and ultimate potential. Don't let your fears rob you of incredible experience that could catapult your career or simply bring joy to your life.

Give thanks for what you have

The simple act of giving thanks has made all the difference in my life. There are many ways you can acknowledge what you're thankful for, but I have found that adding a short morning prayer of gratitude immediately upon waking is a wonderful way to start the day. It takes only a couple minutes, but its effect is enormous.

Put family first

For so many of us, we're too busy in our day-to-day lives to envision the big picture. Family often takes a backseat to work and other obligations. We assume that since they're family, these people will always be around later. But what if later comes too soon? As you put more energy into those individuals most important to you, also remember one of the greatest gifts you can give to another person is to simply say, "I love you!"

Surround yourself with positive people

You may have heard of the law of attraction—the ability of positive thought to bring positive results to your life. The same is true with people. Positive people bring uplifting and positive vibes into your life. Surround yourself with positive people, and their positive energy will spread into your life and allow amazing opportunities to present themselves.

Become a passionate teacher

Part of leading a life of purpose—one full of passion and joy—is to utilize your skills to help others. This could be as intensive as mentoring a group of men or women on a weekly or monthly basis or as simple as sharing your knowledge on a blog or guest posting about something you are passionate about. Find what might work best for you, and give it a try. You may be surprised by just how much you get out of sharing your skills and knowledge with others.

Take care of yourself

When we're healthy, we often take for granted the importance of taking care of our bodies and ourselves. Yet our health greatly plays into our overall happiness, and even small changes can lead to big results. Start by focusing on four core areas: nutrition, exercise, hydration and sleep. And remember, it's never too late to start taking better care of yourself. You are in control of this aspect of your life. You have the option to treat your body well or to abuse it. Make your health a priority.

Live every day like it's your last

Start living the life you want right now! The life you desire is within reach; you just have to grab it and want it. I mean *really* want it. Wake up ready to seize the day and say aloud or in your head, "Today is going to be a great day!", "I'm excited to see where today takes me," or even a simple, "Let's do this!" You deserve a wonderful life—one full of significance, joy and purpose.

Appendix II:
Your Chapter Exercise Cheat Sheet

You Can Have a Better Life was designed to transform your life. But in order to take full advantage of the book and these opportunities for positive change, you need to do two things. First, you need to have an open mind; second, you need to take the time to incorporate the exercises at the end of each chapter into your life.

In most cases, it would be best to implement the lesson immediately following the completion of each chapter; however, I know it's human nature to want to continue reading onto the next chapter. So I've included a Chapter Exercise Cheat Sheet as an easy-to-follow blueprint for your incredible transformation.

I still want to encourage you to pause after each chapter, to take the time to reflect and to implement the lesson whenever you can. But remember that you can also use this cheat sheet to review the exercises at any time.

I can't stress enough how important it is to complete each exercise. Please open your mind and give each and every one of them a try. I know you'll be thankful you did. If you let it, *You Can Have a Better Life* will transform your life!

Chapter 1 Exercise: Believe in Yourself

Set aside five to 10 minutes, find a quiet spot, and give Meditation Release™ a try. Find a quiet place to sit and close your eyes. Allow negative and limiting thoughts to surface; when they do, bring your hands to your head and imagine those negative thoughts to be magnetic and your hands the magnets. Now envision pulling all those limiting thoughts from your mind. Every negative thought flows out of your head and into the palms of your hands; when they've all been removed, pull your hands away and toss those thoughts far from you, letting them dissipate into thin air.

After releasing your limiting thoughts, sit quietly with your palms on your thighs, facing upwards and ready to receive. Think about all the positive thoughts needed to succeed presenting themselves to you. As you sit there quietly with your eyes closed and open palms facing upward, imagine these thoughts materializing in the air around you and falling into your expectant hands. Once all the thoughts have stacked up in your open palms, bring your palms to your head and allow these positive ideas to enter your mind. Imagine these thoughts being pulled into your subconscious and becoming part of who you are.

Chapter 2 Exercise: Don't Wait for Success to Find You

Start by writing down one thing you want to change in your life. It could be something about your job, your finances, your relationship, your health, etc. Then take a few minutes to record three to five actions that will move you in the right direction. Then take it one step further: Under each item listed above, write a specific action that needs to take place for you to succeed. Set a timeframe for each action, and then schedule it into your day.

Chapter 3 Exercise: Visualize Your Success

Set aside an hour of uninterrupted time in the next seven days to create your vision board. Remember to stay true to yourself. No one but you needs to see your work. Once you have your board, post it somewhere you will see it often. If you don't care if others see it, too, I recommend posting it on your bathroom mirror. If you want to keep it private, put it in your sock or underwear drawer where it catches your attention each time you reach in. Most importantly, have fun with the exercise. The activity shouldn't be stressful; it should be motivational.

Once your vision board is complete, make a point of taking just one item from the vision board each day to visualize achieving it. (I suggest right before bed as a great time.) I've found that I can take 60 seconds when I first hop under the covers to do a brief but productive visualization. Remember to make your visualization as specific as possible. Imagine how you will accomplish each goal, see yourself achieving it, and experience the feelings you'll enjoy following your success.

Chapter 4 Exercise: Be All In

Pick an important aspect of your life. It can be your career, a relationship, a personal goal, a skill you're trying to master, etc. Be honest: Are you currently giving this area your all? Are you "all in" or only halfway in? Decide to go for it. Make a list of five actions you can take to ensure you're giving it everything you have. Be all in!

Chapter 5 Exercise: Slow Down to Speed Up

Take some time to assess where you are in your life and what's working and what's not. If something hasn't been working, then step back and analyze why rather than simply pushing harder. It may be that your efforts just need a slight shift in direction. By taking a step back and slowing down for a short period, you give yourself the time needed to evaluate the situation, adjust your course and ultimately succeed.

Chapter 6 Exercise: Never Give Up

Take a minute and think about something you really want to achieve but have encountered obstacles in doing so. Think about the steps you can take to keep moving forward with your dream. And remember, there may be more than one path that reaches your end goal.

Chapter 7 Exercise: See Life as a Gift

Take five minutes and make a list of all the things currently sucking the joy out of your life. Then make another list of all the reasons you're thankful for your life. Take the first list, and just acknowledge each item. Take your second list, the "thankful list," and put it somewhere you can refer to it often (or if it's an electronic file, somewhere that's easy to access). For the next few weeks, review the list on a daily or weekly basis. You can even schedule your "thankful review" into your calendar. I'm confident that the simple act of recording your gratitude and reviewing it often (or even adding to it) will give you a more positive outlook on life.

Chapter 8 Exercise: Practice Self-Acceptance

Every morning for the next 10 days, take 10 seconds after you wake up to say the positive affirmation provided below in front of the bathroom mirror. If you want to make slight modifications, feel free to do so. But if you're struggling with what to say, use the words below.

Morning affirmation: I love the person I am. I am thankful for being alive. I am strong, I am smart, I am beautiful, and I have the power to continue to make positive changes in my life. I am in control of my destiny.

Chapter 9 Exercise: Be Your Real Self

Take a minute to ask yourself these three questions:

1) Are you pretending to be someone you're not?

2) Are you constantly trying to please others but forgetting what's important to you?

3) Is the real you happy?

If you're not being true to yourself, take time to make a list of the things in your life you want to change. This acknowledgement is the first step to creating movement.

Chapter 10 Exercise: Do What Matters Most

Take 15 minutes to write down everything on your to-do list. Include short- and long-term activities, projects, goals, etc. Then number each item from most important to least important.

Once you have your list, determine whether any items can be eliminated by using the three questions discussed in the chapter.

1) Will this task or project improve my life?

2) Will this task or project help me achieve my end goal (one that matters)?

3) If I don't complete this task or project now, will it negatively affect my life?

Next, determine whether anything left on the list can be delegated and set a timeframe to plan for how and when you will transition the activity. Finally, schedule the most important items into your day plan right now. Set aside time for the things that matter most!

Chapter 11 Exercise: Forgive Others

Take five to 10 minutes and review the five steps below to forgiving others.

1) Acknowledge who you want to forgive

2) Acknowledge what was done that caused you pain

3) Let go of the unhealthy obsession that comes with resentment

4) Allow yourself to stop living in the past and to make a fresh start

5) Remember that it's your choice to forgive

Make a plan to move forward by following each step. Ask yourself, "Who do I need to forgive?" Think back on what they did to hurt you. Acknowledge the pain, and then let it go. Then find a way to tell that person you forgive them. It can be face-to-face, over the phone, in a letter or even through a text. It doesn't matter how you do it; what matters is that you let go of the anger you feel toward that person.

Chapter 12 Exercise: Forgive Yourself

Take five to 10 minutes and review the five steps for forgiving yourself.

1) Acknowledge what you've done
2) Take responsibility for your actions
3) Apologize and ask for forgiveness when appropriate
4) Make things right (if you can)
5) Let it go by replacing the guilty thought with a positive one

Decide right here, right now, to free yourself and forgive. Make a plan to move forward by following each step. First, acknowledge what you did. Take responsibility for your actions, and ask for forgiveness. I know that apologizing may be difficult, but it will free you of the guilt currently weighing you down. If you can, try and make things right. Then move on by replacing your guilt with positive thoughts and actions.

Chapter 13 Exercise: Learn From Others

Make a list of three people you'd like to learn from in a face-to-face environment. Call or email them and set up a time to grab coffee or lunch. Also make a list of three people you admire, but most likely can't meet face-to-face. Find a way to connect with them. Follow them on social media or read their blog or book. Schedule time in your calendar to connect. For example, I schedule time to listen to a few people's podcasts. Although they aren't formal mentors and most likely don't even know I exist, I get a great deal out of this virtual mentor relationship.

Chapter 14 Exercise: Have Faith

Take a few minutes every day to quiet your mind and be thankful for what you have right now. If possible, try to schedule this tranquil time—no matter how brief—for the same time each day. This will help you develop a daily habit of taking the time to quiet your mind, be thankful and open yourself to the possibility of good fortune.

Chapter 15 Exercise: Let Go of Fear and Doubt

Spend a few minutes and determine whether fear is holding you back. If so, ask yourself, "What's the worse thing that can happen?" Then go after your dreams!

Chapter 16 Exercise: Give Thanks

When you wake up tomorrow morning, before you even get out of bed, take a few minutes to say a little prayer of thanks. Try doing this for the next five to seven days, and see if it makes a difference. I'm confident it will.

Chapter 17 Exercise: Put Family First

Take a few minutes and tell three people today how special they are. You'll be amazed at how this very quick and simple act can brighten up their day and at the same time bring you more joy.

Chapter 18 Exercise: Surround Yourself With Positive People

Think of the most positive people you know and find a way to spend more time with them. Meet for lunch, or schedule a morning coffee break or happy hour. If this person doesn't live nearby, take the time to connect over the phone or video chat. Reach out today, and make it happen.

Chapter 19 Exercise: Become a Passionate Teacher

If you have the time, make it a priority to mentor a few individuals. If time is too tight, try finding alternative ways to reach out and help people learn from you. And don't forget about the unique opportunities that may exist in your community. Membership clubs, entrepreneurial organizations, schools and so on always have a need for expert advice. Share your knowledge however you can. Not only will others reap the benefits of learning from you, but you will also be amazed at how much you get out of helping others. It's truly a win-win!

Chapter 20 Exercise: Take Care of Yourself

Determine right now how you can make small shifts in four key areas—healthy eating, exercise, hydration and sleep. Start with small changes and build upon them. Pack a healthy snack and carry it with you wherever you go. When hunger strikes, you'll be more likely to make a good choice. Try setting aside 20 minutes to go for a walk, or add five more minutes to your current exercise routine. Start your morning with 24 ounces of water. This will jump-start your water intake and help you reach your daily goal. And lastly, try going to bed 15 minutes earlier today. Continue to add an additional 15 minutes of sleep each night, until you reach a minimum of seven to eight hours. I realize this is a lot to digest at once, but remember that these small shifts take very little time or effort and yield big results! Give them a try.

Chapter 21 Exercise: Live Every Day Like It's Your Last

Make a conscious decision right now to open yourself up to the life you deserve.

Appendix III:
Remembering–A Letter To My Dying Dad

I wanted to thank my dad for everything he did for me and also for making me wake up and embrace the life I still want to live, so I decided to write him a note. This letter to my dad was what first sparked the idea for this book.

It took my dad's deteriorating health and the realization that he wouldn't be with me much longer to make me realize I wasn't living the life I desired. Sitting beside him in the hospital and not knowing how much more time he had left served as my wake-up call. I hope you can relate to this letter and use it to motivate you to go get the life you desire before it's too late.

--- Before Five ---

Dad, I'm trying to remember the early years—those before I was 5—but I'm not sure if the memories I have are real ones, or whether they're simply "memories" from stories I've heard and pictures I've seen.

I'm told you weren't around much during those early years, but I don't remember that. I know now that you were working two jobs, just trying to get by. Already a father to me, and a baby on the way, I'm sure you were worried about how you and Mom would manage. I remember (or I remember hearing) that the landlord of our tiny two-bedroom, one-bath apartment gave us a small folding table so we had somewhere to eat and four metal folding chairs so we had somewhere to sit. I don't remember if we had a sofa then, but I know we had one by the time I was 5, as I saw a picture of me sitting on it with a freshly-molded cast framing my broken arm. I was a tomboy back then and although I thought it was a good idea to swing like Tarzan on the branch of the sizeable yet decrepit tree in our backyard it turned out to *not* be such a good idea.

I know now that when Mom cried as the table and chairs showed up outside our apartment door, her tears weren't 100 percent from joy like she claimed. "Honey," she said, "sometimes people cry when they're happy." Instead, I understand that she shed tears of relief since her family now had somewhere to sit and eat. The table, gifted by someone we barely knew, I now realize was something some adults might view as a handout—something to cause slight embarrassment (even if feeling grateful at the same time). But as a 4-year-old, I only remember the event through a child's eyes: receiving a wonderful gift that was very unexpected.

I'm not sure, Dad, why I'm telling you so much of what I remember at this age. Somehow it seems important to me now—like this is where all my memories of you and mom began. Like this small apartment was the beginning of all my future memories. So here I sit, trying to remember the rest of our humble home. I can visualize the layout of every room. Near the front door, there was a small living space that held our folding table and chairs. Past that, I can see two small bedrooms—yours to the left and mine to the right. The one meager bathroom was closer to my room than yours. Ironically, the kitchen, the room that seemed most important, is also the one I'm having the most difficulty remembering. I can visualize its location, but I only remember how small it was and no other details. That entire kitchen could easily fit inside the space that holds my kitchen island today.

Mom made all our meals in that small space. I remember eating hot dogs and beans often—not because you and

Mom loved them (like I assumed at the time)—but because we couldn't afford much else. I never went hungry.

The only other real memory I have from that time— the time before I became a 5-year-old—involves Mom walking me to preschool. I remember only because the school was right next door to our apartment, with the playground right off our backyard. Mom would walk out to the yard while I was at recess and wave to me, and I'd always excitedly wave back. It's funny how perceptions change. As a kid, I thought living next door to an elementary school—especially one with the playground right off our backyard—was extremely lucky. As an adult, I realize that the close proximity to school wasn't the best feature of our small apartment, but I was happy.

--- Five Years Old ----

At age 5, so many things changed. I remember all the big events of this year, even if I can't remember the minute details. I remember you teaching me how to ride a bike while mom looked on—holding the back of my sparkly silver banana seat and running next to me while I tried to remain upright. I remember you letting go and cheering me on, truly excited for my accomplishment, as I veered off straight into the trunk of the big oak tree that grew out from a sidewalk in front of our place. Fortunately, I wasn't going fast enough to do any damage to the tree, the bike or myself. But I was startled nonetheless, and you came running to my rescue, comforting me and encouraging me to try again (something I would later do with both of my own kids).

Five was a big year. Not only did I learn to ride my bike without the wobbly training wheels, but it also marked many significant life changes for our family. For years I'd been asking for a baby brother or sister, and this was the year you decided to grant this wish and give me one—a little sister. She came into our lives (and into my bedroom), and I got the title I'd been dreaming of: "big sister."

This was also the year during which we moved into a real house. We left the small apartment for a humble (900-square-foot) house, which to me, and in comparison to our previous apartment, felt enormous. The house was more than an hour from our apartment, so I said my goodbyes to all my friends, not knowing I'd never see any of them again. Life as I knew it, in the tiny apartment with the school next door, was over. I was heartbroken, but you and mom were elated.

Our new house in Valencia, a town named for its acres and acres of orange groves, felt monstrous in comparison.

Not only did we have a separate area for our table and chairs, but more importantly (to me), I had my very own room once again. You and Mom even had a bathroom connected to your bedroom rather than out in the hallway to be shared. I remember running all over the house and in and out of each of the three bedrooms. You let me pick my room first, since I was the older sister.

It was strange having our own place. We even had our own front *and* backyard. Although the back remained dirt for some time, the front was vibrantly alive with green grass included with the purchase of the newly built house.

--- Pre-Teen ---

My pre-teen years are full of memories that might hold little significance to an adult, but back then, they felt paramount in my mind. This was the year of "banana butt" (I'll explain later), Del Taco, Dolphin shorts, Kmart and the realization that not everyone lives the same exact way.

As a kid, some seemingly insignificant events unfortunately become the most memorable. We lived only a few miles from the nearest Kmart. This was the only store where I remember ever shopping for school clothes—or anything else, for that matter. In fifth grade, it started to become very important to wear the "right" clothing, which typically cost more than the rest. When it was time to shop before the new school year, I remember begging Mom to buy me the same jeans as the other kids wore. I wanted Jordache, Sergio Valente or even Sasson—name brands that had not yet made it into my closet. But we didn't have the money for these extravagances, so like all previous years, Mom took me to Kmart to stock up on that year's essentials.

When we got to the jeans section, there were no popular name-brands to be found. So I reluctantly opted for two pairs of jeans—the first with a pair of cherries on the back pockets and the second with bananas. The jeans spent most of the summer in layaway, but when it was time for school to start, we paid the last of what we owed and brought the new purchases home. That year, unlike the girls with the perfect hair and cool jeans who were called by their real names, I became known as "banana butt."

I spent many a night crying to Mom about this unfortunate situation. And even after she agreed that I would never have to wear those jeans to school again, the name stuck for nearly the entire year.

The next year, when it came time to go shopping again, Mom took me to lunch at a local fast food restaurant (a very special treat). We chatted over our tacos and burritos and, as we were walking back to the car, she took my hand as we veered toward a popular clothing store that stocked all the newest and most hip clothing brands (like Ocean Pacific and Levi's). I asked Mom what we were doing, as we had never stepped foot in that store before. She said she'd been saving up extra money and wanted to buy me something special. I came out of the store that afternoon with two brightly-colored pairs of Dolphin shorts and my first pair of name-brand jeans. I still remember how great I felt putting on those Jordache jeans, envisioning the memories of "banana butt" slowly fading away.

It wasn't until many years later, when I was in college having a heart-to-heart with Mom, that I learned just how difficult it had been for her to save up enough money for that very special shopping spree. And I know you had something to do with that, too, Dad. Now, as a parent of a 9-year-old daughter for whom I would also do anything to make life easier, I greatly appreciate what you and Mom did for me. (But to this day, I still wish I had been stronger and simply continued to wear my "banana butt" jeans without caring what others thought.)

As I grew, your business did, too. The financial struggles we once faced seemed to slowly disappear—replaced by family vacations, new cars and updated clothing choices. Yet although we were doing well, I know that no matter how hard you worked or how quickly your success came, you continued to compare yourself to your brother.

I know this is a tough subject to address, but I think it's worth a little discussion, even if just to tell you that I would always choose you for my dad. Although I loved my uncle and his big house next to Michael Jackson's—and although a Rolls-Royce parked in a five-car garage, a personal limousine, private chauffer and live-in maid may have been nice—it wouldn't have meant anything without having you as my dad. I realize the financial differences between you and your only sibling didn't make you feel good, but I want you to know that never—not when I was young and not now that I'm nearing 50—did I ever wish to be anyone other than YOUR daughter.

I acknowledge the struggles and dedication it took for you to give us the wonderful life you did. And I have always felt the immense love you showered upon us, as you also taught us more about strength and perseverance than anyone else ever could. I remember being invited to some of those lavish parties that your brother hosted, later listening to their stories about celebrity appearances and feeling somewhat envious of their trips to Europe. Yet, my fondest memories involve the times when our family—you, Mom, me and Michele—enjoyed backyard

BBQs with our neighbors and played at the park pool and later in our own backyard pool, as well as always having you there to tuck me into bed at night. We're the lucky ones!

--- Young Adult ---

As I became an adult, I began to realize just how fortunate I was. Because of you, I was the first person in our family to go to college. I know my enrollment must have been a huge financial burden, but I am forever grateful that you found a way to make it happen and insisted it wasn't a hardship (even though I know it was).

You know I'm a huge believer in education. And although I realize that it may have been possible for me to succeed both personally and financially without a college education, I truly believe those years helped shape my life to make me the successful person I am today. Thank you for your unconditional love and unwavering support.

--- Now You're Dying ---

I can't remember a specific point in time when I realized that your health was deteriorating. The first heart attack came so unexpectedly that we were all caught off guard.

The next three, although always terrifying, didn't seem as surprising. The thought of losing you is not only painful but now also very real. As your health continues to deteriorate, I am trying to face the fact that you, my biggest supporter, may not be with me much longer.

I know you're dying, Dad, but before you go, I want you to know that you made a difference. I know, with certain clarity, that my success is in large part due to what I learned from you. You taught me about perseverance, forgiveness, leadership, hard work and, most of all, you taught me about putting family first. I learned from you that life is short and having fun should be a priority. I learned to always be myself, always believe in myself and always have faith. And I learned that making people laugh (something I'll never be able to do as well as you) is as important as anything else.

My life is richer and I am more successful because of the things I learned by watching you.

Thank you for everything!

I love you!

Dawna

About the Author

D awna Stone is the author of six books and a business owner, entrepreneur, self-made millionaire and motivational speaker. Dawna believes that her Wall Street financial experience and Fortune 500 consulting background helped catapult her entrepreneurial success. Dawna launched the award-winning national magazine *Women's Running* in 2004 and the Women's Half Marathon Series in 2009 (five events across the country— in San Diego, CA; Nashville, TN; St. Petersburg, FL; Minneapolis, MN and Scottsdale, AZ). She sold both companies to the industry leader in 2012.

In addition to speaking all over the country about business success, as a certified health coach Dawna also appears regularly on local and national television shows to share her health and wellness knowledge. Dawna has appeared on *The Today Show*, *MARTHA*, *MSNBC*, *Bethenny*, *HSN* and morning news programs on all four major networks—NBC, CBS, ABC and FOX. She also hosted her own segment on FOX called *Healthy Living with Dawna Stone* and her own radio show on Sirius Satellite Radio called *"Health & Fitness Talk with Dawna Stone."* Dawna regularly writes for popular magazines and websites.

Dawna is a highly sought-after speaker who has fulfilled engagements for an ever-growing list of corporations and nonprofits, including Chobani (Women's Leadership Summit), American Heart Association, Mass Mutual, Wharton Business School, Women's Entertainment Television, PGA Tour, Disney, Super Bowl Leadership Forum, Susan G. Komen, The Crohn's & Colitis Foundation of America, Women in Philanthropy, Bay Care Health Systems and the Snowmass Wellness Expo, to name a few.

Prior to becoming an entrepreneur, Dawna was a financial analyst for Wall Street investment bank Morgan Stanley, a strategy consultant for Deloitte Consulting, the President of a $20 million sports nutrition company, the Senior VP of Operations at a large dot-com and Chief Marketing Officer for a $700 million dollar public-ly-traded company.

In 2005, Dawna competed on and won NBC's *The Apprentice: Martha Stewart*. She spent the following year working closely with Martha Stewart, developing a variety of projects for Martha Stewart Living Omnimedia

Dawna's latest book, *Book Accelerator—How to Write a Bestseller in 16 Weeks: Boost Your Business, Increase Your Income and Get Noticed*, is part of an online and group-coaching program designed to help people publish a book. The work can take readers to the next level in their lives and careers (BookAccelerator.com).

Dawna has an undergraduate degree from UC Berkeley and an MBA from the Anderson School of Business at UCLA. Dawna is also an avid runner and triathlete, having competed in every distance from a 5k fun run to the Hawaii Ironman. She lives in St. Petersburg, Florida, with her husband, 9-year-old daughter, 8-year-old son and 17-year-old "puppy."

To my valued readers,

Thank you for taking time to read *You Can Have A Better Life: 21 Secrets to Getting the Life You Desire—Full of Significance, Joy and Purpose.* I'm confident that if you follow the 21 steps outlined in the book, you can transform your life for the better!

As you may know, it's extremely important to get positive reviews for a book, as it's the best possible way to spread the word about its value. My hope is that *You Can Have a Better Life* will help as many people as possible live the life of their dreams. And you can help! I would be so thankful if you could take a minute to provide an honest review for this book.

Remember, you have the power to get the life of your dreams!

Thank you in advance for your honest review,

Dawna Stone

Free Gift:

As a special thank you for reading *You Can Have A Better Life*, I want to give you two chapters in my next book: *Succeed With Purpose: Unleash Your Potential, Boost Your Career and Increase Your Income.*

**To claim your free chapters, go to:
DawnaStone.com/SWPchapters**

There is no obligation, but if you have a chance to read your free chapters, I would be so delighted to hear your feedback. You can connect with me at Dawna@DawnaStone.com.

www.ingramcontent.com/pod-product-compliance
Lightning Source LLC
Chambersburg PA
CBHW070350070426
42446CB00050BA/2792